Divine Providence

The Mayor, The Mob, and
The Man in the Middle

JEBWizard Publishing
Books with Character

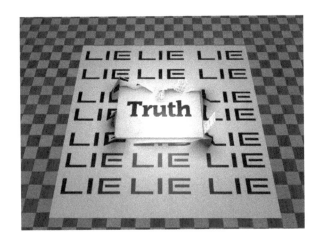

JEBWizard Publishing
Books with Character

Divine Providence

The Mayor, The Mob, and
The Man in the Middle

By Joe Broadmeadow and Pat Cortellessa

JEBWizard Publishing
Books with Character

Printed in the United States of America by IngramSpark

First Printing, July 2021

ISBN Print   **978-1-7368288-2-3**
ISBN eBook **978-1-7368288-3-0**

JEBWizard Publishing
37 Park Forest RD,
Cranston, RI 02920

www.jebwizardpublishing.com

JEBWizard Publishing
Books with Character

Author's Note

The stories within are all true based on eyewitness accounts, interviews, court documents, public records, and news accounts

To protect the privacy of some individuals, some names or locations have been changed.

JEBWizard Publishing
Books with Character

"The first method for estimating the intelligence of a ruler is to look at the men he has around him." ~

Niccolò di Bernardo dei Machiavelli

JEBWizard Publishing
Books with Character

Table of Contents

JEBWizard Publishing
Books with Character

JEBWizard Publishing
Books with Character

Dedication

The book is dedicated to my dad, Pasquale Cortellessa, Sr. A hard-working family man who always put family first.

He was Lorenzo from our Bronx Tale.

Introduction

The echo of the court clerk's announcement of guilty on the Racketeer Influenced and Corrupt Organizations (RICO) Conspiracy count still reverberated in the halls of Judge Ernest Torres' court as the implication ricocheted at the speed of light throughout Providence.

The King is Dead, Long Live the King!

Vincent A. "Buddy" Cianci, the inimitable, affable, yet darkly complex Mayor of Providence, tarnished forever as a now twice-convicted felon. The Providence Renaissance, forever linked to Buddy in fable if not reality, now faced having the curtain pulled back on the myth enveloping the man..

As Shakespeare said, "the evil men do...." The good Buddy would now be buried in the federal prison system, removed from the city he loved almost as much as he loved himself.

All that remained now was for someone to pick up the pieces in City Hall and steer the city forward.

Pat Cortellessa—the once close friend, turned long-time nemesis of Buddy, fresh from the courtroom where he watched the trial and verdict unfold—now stood in city hall with the man who would bear the burden of Mayor, John Lombardi. The scene was surreal, unimaginable just a few short months before. Few expected Buddy to be convicted. Most thought Buddy would emerge dirtied but otherwise unscathed, back in the mayor's office running his domain. Now the celebration of what many viewed as the end of corruption in City Hall was on.

Pat made his way to the mayor's office and walked into what was once the exclusive domain of Buddy. The office, trashed by the celebration, held echoes of so much promise and so many disappointments. Pat wandered over to the window overlooking Kennedy Plaza. The abandoned Café Plaza building, occupying a prominent place in the plaza, the site of so many battles with Buddy, stood as a reminder of the now-former Mayor's penchant for exerting his control wherever he saw an opportunity for self-enrichment.

Pat wondered if it had all been worth it. All those battles fighting for what he believed was right for the city, now mere memories. Buddy was no longer a force to be reckoned with. The conviction took that away. Where it would lead was anyone's guess.

What lay ahead for Pat, he could only speculate. But the memories of the war with the city and Buddy had taken their toll. So how had it all come to this?

This is the story of a mayor who would be King, The Mob, who would demand its share of the kingdom, and a man caught in the middle. A story so unique, so endemic to the city, so uniquely Rhode Island, that it casts a spell even to this day.

And Buddy was now out of sight... but he was far from finished.

Pat Cortellessa Timeline

1977 21 EAST VIP Valet Director/manager

1978 Doorman/Cover charge collector/Ass.t manager Days

1981 Security Chief @ The Gallery

1983 opened Slade's Pub 45 Eddy Street, downtown

1984 partner in NONAME Nightclub downtown Providence

1986 opened River Café
Waterfront district Providence

1990 Opened development of Café Plaza/Comfort station Downtown Providence

1992 Purchased Anthony's Restaurant and Earle Building downtown Providence

1992 Purchased old Corniche Nightclub Downtown Providence

1991 Purchased old Tilly Kings Eddy Street Providence becomes Centerfolds

1992 Purchased building that housed NOBODY café Bassett St.

2001 Purchased Chalkstone House, Providence

2004 Purchased building called Smith St. Pub

1998/2002 Candidate

Mayor of Providence

Beginnings

In the 1950s, Providence, Rhode Island, a gritty, working-class city striving to compete with its big brother, Boston, and not-so-distant cousin, New York, had one thing neither city could claim.

Providence had Raymond L.S. Patriarca, the head of the New England Mob and one of the most respected (among those in the organization) and feared (among those who crossed him) bosses in Organized Crime.

At least in the criminal underbelly and backroom politics, nothing happened in Providence that Patriarca didn't know about, manipulate, control, or profit by. All one had to do was invoke the name, Raymond. No last name or further explanation is needed.

Make no mistake about it, there were two governments in Rhode Island.

Most Rhode Islanders knew *who* Raymond was. Some intimately understood *what* he was. But only a few knew just how far his influential reach extended across the country.

Raymond was more than just a powerful local mob boss. He carried a great deal of influence with the major New York, Philly, and Las Vegas families.

As Pat Cortellessa would come to experience the Patriarca reach for himself—learning even Frank Sinatra had a picture of Raymond L.S. Patriarca in his house in Palm Springs—Raymond was a force of nature. (Stanton, 2003)

When someone like Frank Sinatra, who sang for Presidents, Kings, and Queens worldwide, has your picture on his wall, that should suggest something.

Raymond was no small-time hood from a backwater. On the contrary, Patriarca was a force to be reckoned with, and he cast a shadow over the whole of New England.

Into this world, two men, Vincent Albert "Buddy" Cianci, Jr. and Pat Cortellessa, grew up. While Buddy was fifteen years older, their paths were worlds apart—Cortellessa came from the West end of Providence and went to public schools. Cianci was born into an upper-middle-class family and went to Moses Brown—their lives would be intertwined in ways neither could have imagined.

And the organization controlled by Raymond would cast a shadow over both men.

Pat Cortellessa was born in 1956 and lived on the corner of Chapin Avenue and Messer Street in Providence, Rhode Island. It was a neighborhood of primarily Italian families, triple-decker houses, and neat yards. Where the grandparents were on one floor, and their kid's families lived above them. Even if the family outgrew the house, they didn't move far. Staying in the surrounding streets of the west end of Providence.

When Pat was a kid, an older neighbor, Joe Paris, would load up his car and take the neighborhood boys to the Rhode Island Reds hockey games at the R.I. Auditorium on North Main Street. The Reds played in the old American Hockey League, the original feeder system to the NHL. The days of the Reds playing at "the Arena"—as the place was known—offered kids and adults a chance to see hockey played in all its original, often bloody, glory.

3

No masks, no helmets, few pads. Lots of action between big men on skates, and the only thing separating them from the crowd was a short wall and chicken wire.

No one worried about letting their kids go to the arena. It was a different era in a city and country where World War II was still a powerful memory. The Korean Conflict became the forgotten war. Vietnam was a place few Americans had even heard of, let alone find on a map.

The West end of Providence in the 1950s and 60s was a world away from the east side. Buddy Cianci, already fifteen years old when Pat was born, would attend private school, followed by college and law school. Pat would take a more pedestrian public-school path. Yet their respective careers—politics for one and running restaurants and clubs for the other—would culminate in first a business association, then a friendship, then a break that would drive them both to face each other in the political arena.

One would end up in prison, the other would dance a fine line between the world of the wise guys, the seductive lure of the nightclubs and bars, and the world of politics. Their unlikely association would forever intertwine them in the history of Providence.

But before there was the politics of Cortellessa running against Cianci, there was the Providence Club scene. The payoffs and bribes for liquor licenses, the "rent" paid to the mob for protection, and the always volatile mix of alcohol, pretty women, and testosterone-fueled muscle heads with too much brawn and too under-used brains.

Parking Cars

Like most Providence neighborhoods, the West End was not without its problems. While gangs weren't as notorious or violent as they are now, inter-neighborhood rivalries often erupted.

In 1972, a kid from Federal Hill, nicknamed Cha Cha, bearing the full mantle of the home base of the Mob, beat up a few of the Messer Street guys. He'd come around, challenge a few guys, and punch their lights out. It got so bad, kids would run whenever Cha Cha and some of his crew would show up.

One day, Cha Cha decided it was Pat's turn. He called him on, challenging him to meet at the stairs at the Messer Street School. Not one to back down, a trait that would come to serve him well, Pat accepted.

One lesson bullies often learn the hard way is it is never the size of the man in the fight but the size of the fight in the man. Pat may not have been a muscle-bound gym rat or a polished boxer, but he could fight, and he wasn't afraid.

Cha Cha left with a black eye and a bruised ego. Pat left with a new appreciation he could hold his own in a fight. He learned that it didn't pay to back down. And as he migrated into working the clubs, avoiding confrontations was not always an option.

By 1974, Pat, now eighteen years old, ventured into the Providence Nightclub scene. His first look into a world that would play a big part in his professional business career. But for now, it was just a place to meet women, drink, and jump into the occasional barroom brawl.

These were troubling times in America. The war in Vietnam was essentially over for most Americans— except for those who still had family members there as advisers to the crumbling South Vietnamese military and Government.

The Watergate hearings were mesmerizing the nation as the Nixon Presidency unraveled. When the United States Supreme Court ruled against Nixon in July 1974, compelling him to turn over the tapes recorded in the Oval Office, it was a death sentence to his Presidency. In August, Nixon resigned, and his

Vice-President, Gerald Ford, was sworn in as the thirty-eighth President of the United States.

The following April 1975, Saigon fell to the North Vietnamese Army. The last of the Americans in-country fled aboard helicopters from the top of the temporary U.S. Embassy building.

Americans pushed the bloody, unpopular war and the disgraced Nixon from the headlines. Life in America sought a return to less unsettled times.

With this backdrop, young men like Pat took advantage of one of the war's legacies, the lowered legal drinking age. In 1969, during the height of the American involvement in Vietnam, popular opinion drove changes to the age when young adults could drink. The philosophy was if they were old enough to be drafted and sent to war, they were old enough to sit at a bar and have a beer.

Armed with his legitimate ID, Pat and his friends frequented places like Pisces East. With what was left of his hard-earned money from a job at a milk store after paying for school at Rhode Island Community College, Pat became a regular.

He met the owner Dirk Patriarca's cousin, Angelo. While the owner bore the same name, there was no relation to the more infamous Patriarca of Federal Hill. Angelo owned the Minden Hotel on Brook Street in the Fox Point section of Providence, and Pat often went to the club in the basement. The club featured many fish tanks that gave it a unique atmosphere.

Pat also met the club DJ George, who later would work with Pat at several clubs.

As Pat became more familiar with the club owners and managers, he got offers for side jobs. For example, Dirk Patriarca, trying to convert the former Sheppard's Department Store building into a mall, used Pat for a few minor construction jobs. But the project was never completed, and Dirk Patriarca sold the building.

By 1977, Pat started going to 21 East, a club along the waterfront at 77 India Point. The manager, Roger Gonsalves, asked Pat if he'd be interested in working the VIP parking. Pat jumped at the chance, and his entry into the business side of clubs began.

Working in the VIP parking area, Pat met some rather remarkable characters. A club like this attracted all types.

Politicians and their minions—businesspeople trying to cozy up to the politicians, wiseguys, and the hangers-on living the mob lifestyle vicariously. Popcorn gangsters, as the real mobsters knew them, more movie mobsters than stone killers.

But there were some of the "royalty" of the real Providence mob who frequented the place.

Frank "Bobo" Marrapese, a capo in the Patriarca organization, Gerard Ouimette, a stone killer and close associate of Patriarca although his Irish-French heritage prohibited his full membership, Jerry Tillinghast, an at once intimidating and charming member of Ouimette's crew, Redbird Gomes, once the driver for John Gotti in New York, Matty Guglielmetti another capo with his own crew, and Raymond "Junior" Patriarca, the crown prince of the family still waiting in the wings for his elevation to the boss.

Then there were the guys on the prowl for willing and available young women. The sparcones (Italian American slang for a showy, often gold jewelry adorned male) who would leave their wedding rings in the car believing they were fooling the always observant ladies who pretended to be fooled for free drinks and the occasional parking lot romp, and the usual collection of barflies.

The club rocked and rolled in the money.

The owner of the club—Pete Wilkins—took a liking to Pat and gradually brought him into more important jobs with the business.

Pat would spend four years working his way up from VIP parking to doorman to demolition and club expansion to management. Some of the most unusual moments often happened outside the club rather than inside.

Doormen see more than most in these clubs

In 1977, Bobo Marrapese and his crew were often at the club. Guys like Thomas Pisaniello, Billy Ferle (who in later years would testify against Bobo in two murder trials both ending in not guilty verdicts), Richard "Moon" Diorio (who would also testify against the wiseguys), and others were with Bobo.

Bobo drove a convertible Cadillac Eldorado and had a prominent and reserved parking spot, no matter how crowded the club might be.

One night, Pat sat in the lot listening to the Yankees' game on the radio. He was parked near the door, and people entering the club could hear the game.

Moon Diorio was also a Yankee fan, and Roger Gonsalves, the club manager, was a Red Sox fan. So the two got into what started as a friendly jest about which team was better.

At some point, Roger said, "Fuck off, Moon, the Red Sox are number one."

Moon's mood turned black. Threatening Roger, he said he'd be dead for talking to him like that. Some of Moon's friends intervened and hustled Roger away, defusing the situation. At first, it seemed just another episode soon forgotten.

Three days later, Roger came to the club and packed his stuff. On the way out, he told Pat someone had tried to kill him by running him off the road. Roger never returned to the club.

It would not be the only episode with Moon.

One Sunday night, Moon came in and left his car blocking the boathouse driveway next door. There was plenty of parking in the VIP lot, but Moon loved throwing his mob-affiliated weight around.

On this night, it was also pouring rain. The owner of the boatyard wanted to leave, but Moon's car blocked the driveway. Pat went to Moon and asked him to move the car.

Moon threw the keys at Pat and told him to move the car. Pat said, "No, you do it."

Moon lost his mind. "Do you know who I am?"

Pat didn't back down. When Moon went to move the car, he told Pat, "This ain't over."

The following week, Billy Ferle came in to talk to Pat and find out what happened. After hearing the story, he told Pat not to worry, but he might want to be nicer to Moon, so it doesn't happen again.

On another night, the parking lot was jam-packed. As Pat stood outside in the lot, Jerry Tillinghast, a mob associate of a different crew run by

Gerard Ouimette, came running out of the club chasing someone who'd pissed him off.

With the lot so crowded. Jerry just jumped up onto a car and ran hood to hood to get at the object of his anger. Bobby Allen, the head of security, came out to find out what the problem was. Once Pat told him it was Jerry Tillinghast running on the cars, Allen retreated inside. Whether Jerry ever caught up to the other guys, Pat never found out. Shortly after this incident, Jerry Tillinghast went to jail for murder. The club closed long before he ever got out thirty-three years later.

Just another night in the world of mobsters and music clubs in the Providence of the 1970s and 80s.

By 1981, Pat would move on from 21 East after things got even crazier. Internal problems between the owners and Bobby Allen and friends made things dicey. Instead of settling beefs with fists, weapons showed up. Life inside was getting dangerous, and it was time to move on.

Parallel Paths: The Rise of Buddy

On January 7, 1975, while Pat Cortellessa was learning the ropes on both sides of the bar, then thirty-three-year-old Vincent A. "Buddy" Cianci was sworn in as the Mayor of Providence for his first term. Buddy may not have planned the irony, but he ran on an anti-corruption campaign, having worked as a prosecutor with the Rhode Island Department of Attorney General's Anti-Corruption Task force.

In 1972, before his political career took shape, Buddy was the assistant prosecutor in the re-trial of Raymond L.S. Patriarca on murder conspiracy charges. After a bizarre trial involving perjured testimony by a defense witness, who was a Catholic priest and, as it would come to light decades later, perjured testimony by the star witness for the prosecution, John "Red" Kelly, a bank robber and killer, and FBI agent H. Paul Rico, who lied to corroborate Kelly's testimony, Patriarca was found not guilty.

There's a legendary story of Cianci sitting at a table at a restaurant in Federal Hill, listing out the pros and cons of two life-altering choices. One was to buy a boat; the other was to run for Mayor.

In hindsight, he should have bought the boat.

Cianci's entangled web with the mob started with them on opposite sides of the law, but time would weave them together in a more symbiotic relationship. Running for office in Providence required reaching out to the various neighborhoods. While Federal Hill was the center of the mob universe, places like Silver Lake and other areas had their share of wise guys.

Politics not only makes strange bedfellows, but it often bears stranger progeny.

Wise guys ran certain neighborhoods and controlled the local ward bosses. The only way to gain their votes was to make overtures. Jobs were promised, neighborhood improvements offered, and votes were gathered.

Gerard Ouimette and some of his associates gathered absentee ballots for delivery to the Cianci side. It was politics at its local best, and Buddy was a quick study. Bringing traditional Democrats and Republicans into a coalition supporting an independent candidate against Incumbent Mayor Joe Doorley and the Irish-led Democratic machine was no mean trick. Convincing Ouimette and crew to swing their support was a masterful stroke.

Yet Buddy wasn't the only candidate who came seeking votes from the wiseguys. A candidate for the state senate once sought ought similar support for his initial run. For his first election, Ouimette and crew delivered votes as promised but soon soured on the candidate when he proposed re-instituting the death penalty for murder. Such legislation was anathema to groups where murder was a method of eliminating problems.

Even the mob had a political platform, and they always opposed the death penalty. Irony doesn't even come close.

Buddy knew better than to bite the hand that fed him, allocating plenty of city jobs to the wiseguys. Several of the more infamous to work for the city were a who's who of mob connections.

William "Blackjack" DelSanto, a made member of the Patriarca family, Jerry Tillinghast, one member of Gerard Ouimette's crew, Edward "Buckles" Melise, an associate of Frank "Bobo" Marrapese, a capo in the Patriarca organization, and others often had city jobs of questionable need. Some actually worked, some just pretended to, but they continued to support Buddy to maintain their jobs.

It would be in this auspicious beginning to a political career. Buddy Cianci would rise from being the mayor of the smallest big city to the national stage, to consideration as Gerald Ford's VP candidate, to giving an address at the Republican national convention in 1980.

These were heady times for the kid from the east side of Providence. But dark clouds loomed on the horizon, and the even darker psyche of the mayor would soon rise to the forefront of the news.

The mayor's first few terms were a preview of the coming controversies.

From employee strikes to financial hardships to a long-running battle with the state over control of the waste management system, the mayor was often in the news.

During one confrontation, where the mayor wanted to privatize garbage collection, city employees went on strike. The mayor sent shotgun-toting police officers to literally ride shotgun on private contractor garbage trucks. He later claimed the guns weren't loaded.

The strike turned into a disaster for the union and a huge political win for the mayor. The handling of the strike made Buddy a hero within the city, at the cost of the animosity of the union workers, but he later ameliorated the bad feelings.

This led to more complex financial situations within the city.

One of the more colorful episodes that played out in the media was the battle between the city and the state to take over the wastewater management system

Episodes like this are often forgotten in the blazing light of the Cianci personality.

And bear in mind, these were during Buddy's first terms. The tone was set long before Plunder Dome got started.

During the often-contentious struggle with the state over control of the wastewater treatment facility, some curious arguments were presented by Ronald Glantz and Robert Chase representing the city.

> *"The city downplayed the importance of the fecal matter dumped into the bay as a result of the plant breakdown. Both claimed that the heavy metals passing through the system, into the plant (thereby disrupting the biomass) and out into the bay bottom muck was a bigger problem. (The heavy metals mostly come from the state's jewelry industry).*
>
> *Heavy metals certainly are regarded as a major source of Bay pollution. Yet to pretend that raw sewage is not a big problem when it is dumped into public waters is a grotesque position. * (Haupt, 1982)*

When the Providence Journal published a story about the fecal material being dumped into the bay as a result of failure in the system, Glantz reportedly said, "Shit doesn't hurt fish, fish digest it." (Haupt, 1982)

Cianci faced a difficult political position. Almost everyone hated the idea of new taxes, while only a smaller percentage of voters cared about the stuff getting dumped into the bay.

Finding the money to fund repairs would require new taxes, appeasing a few environmentalists and angering most taxpayers.

While the wastewater drama played out, the city faced an even more severe financial crisis. The reality was the city was on the verge of bankruptcy. Bills weren't getting paid, they were in danger of not making payroll, banks were placing significant conditions on the usual routine short-term loans to cover the gaps, and none of the solutions were palatable.

In 1981, the Providence Review Commission took over the city's finances. They recommended a supplemental tax levy to stabilize the city. Facing the real prospect of financial failure, the mayor had no choice but to support the measure.

The public reaction was, as expected, overshadowing the wastewater issue. And while this city matter played out in the public eye, a different storm was gathering in the mayor's private life.

In 1984, Buddy's personal life collided with his political life. Incensed by rumors of an affair between his then-wife, Sheila, and Bristol business executive Raymond DeLeo, Cianci summoned DeLeo to his Power Street home and confronted him.

What transpired inside the home is a thing of legend. One of the most troubling stories in Rhode Island lore. Cianci, with the help of his driver, a Providence Police Officer, held DeLeo captive, threatening him at various times with a lit cigarette and a fireplace log.

Persuaded by the calmer heads of friends, Cianci eventually let DeLeo go, but the damage was done. DeLeo went to the police, charges were brought, and Cianci, faced with the prospect of conviction and potential jail time, entered a plea of nolo contendere to the assault.

He received a five-year deferred sentence and resigned from the mayor's office.

But he was far from finished. Joining the talk show circuit, he built a radio talk show on WHJJ-AM into the most popular show in Rhode Island. Always the showman, Cianci took on the politicians and public figures with the same zest and cutting humor as he did politics.

Among his many callers was "Ray from Lincoln," who many are convinced was Raymond "Junior" Patriarca, the son and heir to the mob kingdom of Raymond L.S. Patriarca, Sr., and a host of other notable and not-so-notable followers of the show.

Cianci, whose quick mind, wit, and limitless ability to ignore criticism, commanded the coveted after-work drive time slot on the airways for almost seven years.

Among the many celebrities Cianci charmed was none other than the late Don Imus, the irreverent, often controversial New York talk show host

Imus referred to Cianci as the "thug mayor," but Cianci held his own in the battle of acerbic wits.

Cianci seemed to have the ability to fall into a sewer in front of a cheering audience yet pull himself back out to an even louder standing ovation.

Most men driven from office under a cloud of criminal behavior would forever avoid the limelight. Cianci was drawn back to it like an addict to his drug of choice.

In 1990, fresh off his deferred sentence, Cianci did what many thought inevitable. While Buddy's loyal followers never wavered, his margins of election victory never approached fifty percent of votes cast. Under the city's election rules, whoever got the most votes won. In his earlier bid for office, Buddy merely edged out the other candidates. Most voters voted for other candidates, just not enough for one candidate to defeat Cianci.

Running again to reclaim the office he had given up by resigning was thought, by most, impossible. But this was Providence, Rhode Island, where the public loved the underdog. And given Buddy's charismatic charm, penchant for remembering people's names, and experience with the darker side of Providence politics, no one doubted if anyone could pull it off, it would be Buddy.

And, of course, he did. He would reclaim the office and become one of the longest-serving mayors of a "big" city in the United States, serving from January 1991 through September 2002.

In April 2001, the death knell of the second reign of Buddy Cianci reverberated throughout the city. Operation Plunder Dome, a widespread corruption investigation by the U.S. Attorney's Office, the FBI, the Rhode Island State Police, aided by the undercover cooperation of Providence businessman Antonio Freitas, brought indictments under the Racketeer Influenced and Corrupt Organizations Act (RICO) against Cianci and several members of his administration including conspiracy, solicitation of bribes, extortion, and other charges.

What most didn't know was the FBI first approached Pat about working undercover. Pat told them that he could divert Buddy's attention to raising money for the campaign and increase the potential avenues of corruption by running for office. He wanted to take the public role of targeting the mayor's corruption.

Cianci would stand trial and be convicted on one count of the RICO indictment. Many were shocked, some were distraught, others, among them Pat Cortellessa, relieved that justice had finally caught up with Cianci's corruption and criminal actions.

The once and former mayor would be sentenced to five years in federal prison. The resurrected career of Vincent A. "Buddy" Cianci shattered by the inevitability of corrupt acts.

For Pat Cortellessa, this was a moment of mixed emotions. From the opening of Pat's club, Slade's Pub, in 1983, where he first became acquainted with Buddy and built a friendship and business relationship, to the betrayal by Cianci, the political backbiting, the dissolution of a friendship, and the vindictive attack by the mayor and others on Pat's businesses, this moment was the culmination of years of determination to see justice done.

Pat spent many days of the trial sitting in the courtroom. After Freitas testified, they often sat together. While they awaited the jury when they reported a verdict, Pat had a direct view of Buddy at the defense table.

One thing stands out in his mind from that moment. As the jury filed in, Cianci's hand, gripping a pen, shook incessantly.

It was, perhaps, a moment of realization on Buddy's part that maybe, just maybe, all those incidents in the past, where his ambition and greed overruled his intelligence and talents, were about to exact a price.

When the guilty verdict was announced, the elation among those who'd been the object of Buddy's vindictive side was like an earthquake. Yet the full story of what transpired from those hopeful days in 1983 to the jury's verdict in 2002 is a most troubling, complex story.

One littered with missed opportunities and squandered chances.

What began with such high hopes and expectations became the stuff of nightmares and self-preservation.

From the Gallery to Arson at the East Side Diner, to Slade's and the River Cafe

In March 1981, things got dangerous at 21 East. Bobby Allen, then head of security, brandished weapons to intimidate problem customers. Pat could see the writing on the wall. Remember, this was in the cocaine-fueled insanity of the time when weapons, alcohol, testosterone, and dominance-seeking males often considered a night without a fight a failure.

It was only a matter of time before Pat witnessed a murder, got caught in the crossfire, or ended up with the impossible choice of testifying against wise guys or facing criminal charges himself.

Salvation arrived in an opportunity. Pat built a reputation of diffusing a situation when possible and controlling a security crew that could handle those situations where words were replaced by fists. He could navigate the often dangerous and uncharted waters of tough guys, mobsters, and the club environs.

It had not gone unnoticed.

Roland Lemonthe, the manager of the Gallery Nightclub, faced a dilemma. While wildly successful as one of the first openly gay clubs in the city, the club was on probation and faced a potential loss of its liquor license if it didn't stop the fights and violence. So Lemonthe tried to take the club in a new direction, turning it into a popular disco in keeping with the times, but he needed help.

Roland approached Pat and offered him the security job. From Pat's perspective, it was an easy decision. While the wise guys often came into the Gallery, Pat rarely had a problem with them. It was the idiots and wannabes who might not know the guy sitting at the bar checking out his girlfriend was a capo in the mob.

The mob guys always had a piece of most clubs in Providence and were there not just for the drinks and music. They were there to monitor their investments and remind the owner and manager to toe the mark or face the consequences.

This was something Pat had seen up close and personal at 21 East, so it was a simple transition.

However, the reality of doing business in Providence foreshadowed what Pat would experience doing business with another form of organized crime, City Government, under a certain mayor.

Pat knew how to spot problems before they began and how to derail them before the cops showed up. He took the job and moved on from 21 East.

Like every club, this one had its problems. Certain guys felt they could do whatever they wanted, and it created the usual troubles. While Pat got the club through its probation period, the inevitable fights and disturbances continued.

Pat had an incident with another wise guy, a long-time mob associate and enforcer, who made his bones with the mob when he took the beef for an arrest involving another made guy. He once worked in the place but was no longer employed there.

The wise guy was a loose cannon. He came into The Gallery right after getting out of jail and got into a fight using a pool cue and a blackjack he always carried.

Pat had to make it stop.

30

He confronted him, and a fight ensued. Pat got the upper hand. But winning a fight rarely ended the problem.

Pat knew, with the guy's connection, he might try to get the nod to take Pat out. Pat reached out to the wiseguys and explained he was just protecting the club. A club that, Pat reminded them, was making them money.

Cooler heads prevailed, and they told the guy to let it go.

This problem was solved. But when dealing with these guys, one was never sure it was over. Loyalty is a fleeting phenomenon in this world.

At one point, it got so bad Pat resorted to keeping an M-1 carbine in his car, just in case. Not so much because of this incident—Pat had faith in mob diplomacy and the word of Bobo Marrapese—but the sometimes violent, alcohol-fueled idiocy that infested the nightclub scene. While the occasion never called for him to use it, it was reassuring by its mere presence.

In May 1981, a new presence showed up in The Gallery as an employee in charge of "security.". Bobo Marrapese, fresh out of prison, made himself known there on weekends.

The FBI found out about the situation, and two agents approached the owner, Bob Thibeault, to see if Bobo was shaking the place down.

Bob told them Bobo was on the payroll and was staying on it no matter what they said. Thus, a new element to the already circus-like environment entered the picture.

Seeing the effect of having guys like Bobo around made an impression on Pat. Roland seemed to know keeping a guy like Bobo on the payroll could go a long way to mitigating problems from outside and inside. He knew the wiseguys protected their territory.

And having some tough guys inside to deal with the knuckleheads trying to prove their invincibility by starting fights couldn't hurt either.

There were no referees in these fights, no Marquis of Queensbury rules to these often-bloody conquests.

These guys fought to win by ending the conflicts quickly, whatever it took.

Bobby Walason, one of Bobo's toughest associates, sometimes worked the door at the Gallery. Walason was a natural boxer, powerfully built, and fearless.

He was also a fan of nice clothes. One of the biggest problems with being a bouncer was the bloodstained clothing he often left the club wearing, courtesy of another mistaken tough guy.

While guys like Walason never lost the battle, it could get expensive replacing all the torn shirts, ripped off buttons, and blood-covered jackets, which were a common feature of the job.

Most of the nightly—and they were almost nightly—incidents have faded from memory, but a few still stand out in Pat's mind.

The benefit of hindsight now shows how some seemingly unrelated events may have sparked some severe repercussions.

One night in the Gallery, a Rooster's employee (the former 21 East, which had closed less than a year after Pat left) got into a beef with a friend of the club named Dino Pacia.

Dino was Bobo's cousin, so there was the added drama of that connection. Pacia never asked for any help because of his cousin; it just hung there like an avenging angel.

Ferle constantly mistreated Pacia, even as a youngster. Once Pacia became an adult, Ferle's mistreatment never stopped.

It was never anything too severe—once he took a match to Pacia's jacket in the Gallery—but he made it clear he didn't like Pacia.

Dino kept clear of Ferle as much as he could. He wanted no part of the wiseguy crowd—he just enjoyed going to the various clubs—and he avoided associating with his cousin's crew as much as possible.

But Ferle took every opportunity he could to torment the young man. Perhaps it was jealousy of the relationship with Bobo. On the other hand, Ferle was just the hired muscle, he wasn't there because he qualified for Mensa, and he wasn't *family* in any sense of the word. His job was the pure application of brawn. He didn't have to know how to spell.

He did once tell Pacia, "Someday, I might forget your Bobo's cousin."

But he never did. Instead, he testified against Bobo. But all of that was still to come. For now, he was just an annoyance.

This situation—a minor beef in a crowded club—was handled with the usual alacrity by the security staff.

Pat and several other security guys escorted the Rooster's employee out. During the scuffle, his Roosters jacket came off. Pat held onto the jacket as a keepsake.

Pat called Bobby Allen at Roosters to tell him to keep his people out of the Gallery. The call was also to put them on notice this nonsense wouldn't be tolerated. They would meet force with greater force.

The call was not well received, but it sent the message. Time has allowed Pat to reflect on what the call may have provoked.

Shortly after this incident, the firebombing happened at the East side diner site. This inter-club rivalry was intense and getting worse.

Several weeks later, there was another incident. One of Bobo Marrapese's nephews was dancing at Roosters. An argument broke out with one of the bouncers, and he threw Bobo's nephew out.

"Go get you fucking uncle; I don't give a fuck." The bouncer said.

So the nephew did.

Bobo and his crew were inside the Gallery when the nephew told him the story. Pat watched with amusement as Bobo and several very tough guys jumped in their cars and paid a visit to Roosters.

Walking in the club, they didn't bother paying the cover charge but went right to the office to confront the bouncer.

What happened inside is anyone's guess, but when they returned to the Gallery, Billy Ferle tossed the deadbolt from the office door at Rooster's onto the bar.

Two other memorable incidents that happened inside the club didn't involve any other rival club.

In May 1982, there was an incident at the Fidas restaurant in Providence. A confrontation between Bobo, Billy Ferle, and Anthony "the Moron" Mirabella ended with Mirabella being shot to death.

Several weeks later, the news media reported a body found in a swampy area of Warwick with several bullet holes and described as wearing high-top sneakers.

That night, Bobo and Ferle were in the Gallery. One of the bouncers pulled up the leg of his pants, pointed at his sneakers, and joked, "Hey Billy, high-tops!"

Ferle yelled at the bouncer. "What are you, a fucking stupid idiot?"

Bobo just kept enjoying his cigar and shook his head at the nonsense.

The joke was not well received, but nothing more than angry words was exchanged.

Ferle would later testify at Bobo's murder trial in the Mirabella murder. They would find Bobo not guilty. Ferle would also testify about another murder, 20-year-old Ronal McElroy, beaten to death with a bat.

The incident with McElroy and two other young men was particularly gruesome. Bobo and Bobby Walason were driving in Bobo's car when a Volkswagen cut them off.

The three young men in the car then flipped off Bobo when he laid on the horn.

Bobo got on the car's bumper and tapped them a few times. Finally, the car pulled into a parking lot, and the three men got out with bats and clubs.

While Walason fought off two of the men—they had no idea the nightmare they'd just stepped into—eventually chasing them off, Bobo took on the guy with the bat.

Billy Ferle, who'd been behind Bobo, pulled up and wrestled the bat from McElroy. He later testified that Bobo had beaten McElroy to death, but the jury didn't believe him.

Bobo would be acquitted of that murder as well.

Needless to say, once Ferle began cooperating with the State Police, he was no longer welcome at the Gallery.

In another gem of a night, Pat recalled a potentially serious problem that would have made national news but for a lucky break.

Pat recalled the incident.

"Sometimes Patriots players would come to the Gallery nightclub on Sunday night after the game. One night, Marrapese comes over to me at the door and says, 'If Andre Tippett comes in, I will beat the tar out of him.'

I asked why what happened? Bobo says my wife has a dress shop on Atwells Ave, and Andre was disrespectful to her—meaning he flirted with Marie.

"As the night went by, I was hoping Andre and any other Patriots did not show up. Thank God. The clock struck 1:00 A.M., and we closed. No Patriots ever came back to the nightclub again."

While these incidents have some element of humor in them, they were wearing Pat down.

Pat wanted something more than these daily headaches and problems. He wanted his own place.

But where?

In June 1982, Ron Rainey drove by the old Jimmy's East Side Restaurant on Waterman Street just before the Henderson Bridge to East Providence.

In the business's window was a sign advertising the building for rent with contact information for Harold Shine Realty Company.

Ron talked to Pat, and they decided to go for it.

Managing a business was one thing; owning the company was an entirely different animal. Pat would soon learn the world of business had a dark underbelly in Providence. And while there were never any overt demands, the wink and a nod of backroom deals were as clear as any direct overture.

Security by the mob was known as "Piece of Mind Security." We get our piece; you get to keep your mind.

Ron Rainey—whose cousin was Billy Ferle, then a member of Bobo Marrapese's crew and a dangerous guy who ultimately turned government witness after an arrest for arson in New Hampshire—and Pat put together some money—including 10K from Pat's father—and started renovating the place which they planned to call Humphrey's.

Knowing that opening a club in the city would draw attention from the competition and suspecting this could pose problems unless properly managed, Pat told Rainey to do two things. Both involved insurance plans.

He gave Rainey a check to buy traditional business insurance. Then, he told him to arrange a less conventional but equally necessary type of insurance. Pat wanted Rainey to contact his cousin Billy Ferle to pass on to Bobo they would be welcome to put their vending machines in the club.

Business insurance is always wise. Wise guy insurance is ever wiser.

On August 31, 1982, just weeks before finishing the renovations, disaster struck. And it was anything but natural.

41

Arsonists burned the place, totaling the building and Pat's business plan.

After surveying the damage, Pat asked Rainey about the insurance. Turned out, he had done neither.

Pat was content with letting it go. However, he knew there was a message here and had his suspicions about who sent it. So he approached Bobo and told him, "A man had the right to earn a living."

Bobo said he would look into it.

Later, Ferle told Pat, without directly mentioning the location, "Bobo looked into it. He said it wasn't personal. And next time, come to him before you buy a club, and he will make sure nobody does anything."

The message was clear. For whatever reason—a beef with the building owner, lack of an offer to put their machines in the business, or just eliminating club competition—someone burned the building. So Pat's investment went up in smoke.

Pat had his suspicions, but no one was ever charged.

Resigning himself to the inevitable, Pat removed his furniture and equipment from the damaged building.

No one showed up to help.

Pat took the lesson to heart, vowing to handle any future business ventures differently. The clubs were all infiltrated by the mob. The only way to do business was to manage that complication and avoid the problems of other jealous club owners.

Pat recalled those days. "I knew I had to find a way. I am a student of military history, and it reminded me of the non-aggression treaty between Germany and the Soviets. To invade Poland without the Russians interfering, Hitler made the pact.

"From my perspective, I was in the same situation. To open a business, I had to keep the wiseguys at bay."

Pat accepted the lesson and went back to the Gallery.

By 1983, the drama of working clubs for others took its toll. Things were crazy in the Gallery since

Bobo, who asserted some control, left for prison in February 1983.

It was time for Pat to look for his own place. On the corner of Washington and Eddy Street and owned by Providence business executive Charles Krasnoff, the Slade building offered such an opportunity.

After some negotiations, raising 25k in seed money, and a 50k loan, Pat leased space in the building and opened Slade's Pub. This is where Pat's experience with the behind-the-scenes- reality of owning a club in Providence came into play.

Pat took that experience and put it into practice.

In attendance at the grand opening was the Mayor, Buddy Cianci. It was said of Buddy he would attend the opening of an envelope, and true to form, he entertained the crowd with his quick wit.

Among those charmed by the charismatic Cianci was Pat Cortellessa.

"Buddy was a charmer," Pat recalled. "He had a way of making you feel like you were the center of his attention. He did it for everyone yet made you think he was focused on you.

"I had been told Buddy was someone to have on your side, so I made a point of getting to know him. Buddy also met Charles Krasnoff, the building owner. At one point, I watched Buddy and Krasnoff go outside and engage in a bit of a heated argument. Kransnoff never said what the argument was about, so I just let it go."

Later, Ronald Glantz, an associate of Krasnoff and onetime lawyer for the city, would be indicted and convicted on various criminal charges related to extortion and other nefarious activities. In addition, there were allegations of fraudulent use of Housing and Urban Development funds for building renovations in a Krasnoff property never completed. On the second floor of the Slade building, the Narragansett Bay Commission had office space. No one ever worked there, and it was mainly used for storage.

Part of the allegations against Glantz concerned a now-defunct corporation, Eticam, which purportedly imported Foreign Waste Disposal Technology and a second company formed to seek financing for Eticam. Both companies were connected to Glantz and suspicious property transactions involving building a sewer treatment facility for the City of Providence.

While there was never any direct connection between this matter and Cianci (Glantz had left working for Cianci in 1981), one must wonder if the argument between Buddy Cianci and Krasnoff was tied to Glantz's activities. In court records in 2002, Glantz alleged Cianci received cash payoffs from a R.I. businessman for contracts by the City to buy garbage trucks.

This backroom dealing would not come to light until much later. So, it was without the benefit of knowing the inner workings of the Cianci organization that Pat began as a cordial relationship with the mayor until it deteriorated into a political and personal war between the two men.

One who would rise from the ashes of a political disaster of his own making to regain the office and mayor and one who, armed with the experience of seeing the real Buddy in action, tried to derail the Cianci juggernaut.

But all this was in the future; for now, Pat settled into the world of running a string of nightclubs in the city.

"Buddy started coming in Slade's for a drink once in a while. Sometimes, he'd bring his daughter, Nicole, and while Buddy sat at the bar, she'd play the Pac-Man video game.

In 1983, Roland Lamonthe left the Gallery—which was closed because of repeated disturbances, assaults, and robberies—and became the manager at Slade's.

But Pat maintained control overall.

Knowing that the club would attract the attention of the wiseguys, Pat contacted Tom Pisaniello. He ran the day-to-day operation for Bobo Marrapese's Video Games and Pool table business.

"Bobo Marrapese owned the video games and pool tables. It served as a safety net from jealous nightclub owners. Using those machines was insurance against the business burning to the ground, as I knew from personal experience. Of course, Coin-O-Matic (the business front controlled by Raymond L.S. Patriarca) had the cigarette machines.

Using the machines from these guys didn't cost the business anymore—each side got 50% of the proceeds—but using the wiseguys machines had other fringe benefits.

Regrouping, Pat focused his efforts on making Slade's successful and kept his eyes open for opportunities.

In 1984, the No Name Disco operated on the second floor of a building on Weybosset Street and Dorrance Street owned by Joseph Paolino, Sr., father of the future Mayor of Providence. Because of a business dispute, Paolino padlocked the business. He was owed back rent. The owner, desperate to get his business reopened, needed a solution.

The business owner came to Pat looking for help. Pat's reputation as a solid club manager and business owner was spreading. Pat offered to buy in for 50% of the business. The former owner would become a silent partner to satisfy Paolino, who initially demanded the owner gone. Pat brought in Peter Wilkins (from 21 East) as an investor. Eventually, Ron

Rainey bought him out. However, the old nonsense from the past just wouldn't go away.

In late 1986, Pat was ready to take on a new endeavor. He made Ron Rainey the full owner through a purchase and sale agreement to buy Pat's interest in the location.

Pat then opened the River Café in Providence. He would turn the River Café into his most successful business. Still, it was not without its problems., with the potential to turn very violent.

A String of Clubs

Pat opened the River Café at 556 South Main St. Shortly after opening, DJ George, one of the most popular DJs in Providence, had enough of the nonsense and fights at his current club, Roosters. Pat approached DJ George about coming to work at The River Café. George jumped at the chance—a DJ with a vast following was a guaranteed draw and can make a club successful.

With DJ George in place, business at River Café boomed. The owners at Roosters were not pleased. One night, a competition club owner with some of his muscle-bound bouncers showed up threatening to break the DJ's hands. Guns were flashed—one of the club owners has a carry permit and made of show of letting everybody see the gun—and they told Pat they were taking DJ George out.

Pat, retrieving his own weapon and gathering his own security team, challenged the group. After several tense moments of threats, counter-threats, and bravado, the Rooster's crew withdrew, and DJ George stayed put with his fingers intact.

Pat once again reached out to Bobo Marrapese through Thomas Pisaniello, and the matter was resolved. DJ George would stay with Pat. While satisfied the matter was handled, Pat kept a wary eye on the DJ and the club, making sure no one created problems.

While the inter-club rivalry—sometimes escalating into confrontations—was a constant, it was just background noise to Pat's successful club career.

Among the many successful ventures held at the club, one involved an enterprising force of nature named Billy "Billy V" Vigeant.

Billy V was an entrepreneur in the most refined sense of the word. After a brief sports career ended by an unfortunate injury, Billy V created a series of successful business ventures.

One of these ventures became wildly popular. It was called V.I.G.—Very Important Guy, Very Important Girl.

Clients would get the star treatment—limo rides, VIP treatment at clubs, hobnobbing with sports and entertainment celebrities, a night to remember.

V.I.G. became so popular, Bob Kerr, a Providence Journal reporter, wrote a story about the night he was given the V.I.G. treatment. He spent the night riding around the city with Boxing Champion Vinny Pazienza, Leon from Dayton Tire, and Rapper Bobby Braciole, visiting various clubs, and living the life of a rock star if only for that one glorious night.

That was the V.I.G. treatment, and it played a big part in Pat's club success. (Broadmeadow, Legendary Speaking, 2021)

It made quite a story in the Journal, highlighting some of the best aspects of the club atmosphere Pat created within his various locations.

Mostly, things stayed quiet. But there was an incident that came close to derailing the ceasefire and plunging the place back into chaos.

The Night the Glass Eye Rolled Down the Stairs

In the world of nightclubs, there are certain inevitabilities—fights and the need for bouncers to control them. Pat ran a diverse group of bouncers in his clubs. They had to know how to fight, size helped with the intimidation factor (although some saw it as a challenge), but Pat wanted guys who could contain the violence without escalating it through overkill.

Jimmy Vickers was one of Pat's guys. Pat had confidence in both Jimmy's ability and self-control. Yet everyone has a bad day.

One day, Jimmy and another very tough guy, Kevin Hanrahan, an enforcer for the Patriarca Crime family, collided on their bad day. Unfortunately, Kevin ended up worse off than Jimmy. Jimmy almost ended up another victim of violent mob retribution.

Pat hired Jimmy away from the original Lupo's Heartbreak Hotel to run the bouncing crew at River Café. They had been friends for years, but truth be told, bouncers do it for the money. Jimmy was no different. Pat matched Jimmy's Lupo's salary and added more nights.

Jimmy's loyalty was to the money, not where he earned it, so he came to work for Pat.

River Café didn't succeed right out of the gate. The club struggled until they hired DJ George. After that, it was overcrowded every weekend. Pat convinced the Fire Marshall to raise the occupancy limit, jamming more people in. But overcrowding, poor ventilation, and alcohol are a recipe for problems. It meant a good three of four fights every night.

The night Kevin Hanrahan came in, Jimmy wasn't working; he was injured from his straight job at Almac's warehouse. He'd gotten hurt defending the President of Teamster's 251, John "Jackie" Amaral, during a union hall brawl. These were colorful days in Jimmy's world, but the colors were about to go dark.

The details are lost to the fog of memories and the inevitable alterations of such things by time. Still, Pat recalled some details of that night.

Once Vickers and Hanrahan got into it, Pat separated them. As he was leading Hanrahan away, Hanrahan took a sucker shot at the bouncer. This triggered the already hyped-up security crew, and they pummeled Hanrahan for hurting their fellow bouncer.

Hanrahan was hurt, lost his glass eye during the scuffle, and was last seen still raging as friends dragged him away.

Pat told Vickers to clear out, and he'd handle the mob guys. Later that evening, Bobby Almonte, another wiseguy, who'd been with Hanrahan earlier, returned to retrieve the lost eye.

The next day, Chippy Scivola, a respected and feared member of the Patriarca family, called Pat to find out what happened.

Pat did his best to smooth it over, portraying the beef as a barroom brawl and nothing more. He hoped it would be enough to prevent anybody from ending up in a shallow grave.

Jimmy recalls the aftermath of the incident.

"I didn't know until the following day when Pat called me that it was Kevin Hanrahan. Pat wanted me to go to a Federal Hill sit-down and squash the whole thing.

"Pat's reasoning was that it was his club, and Bobo was his guy. They came into his joint and started a beef with us. Seemed reasonable on paper. But I took a quick inventory of the fact that I'm not Italian, and had less skin in the game than Hanrahan, less value. If push came to shove, Pat could get overridden, even though he was well respected. Or, tempers could flare, and Hanrahan could shoot me. He wasn't known as a level-headed killer.

"The 'made' guys told Kevin they wouldn't sanction my murder or even a beating. Instead, they sided with Pat, agreeing it was a beef between two guys, a bar fight, period. Pat called me later and told me that. I told Pat, 'Just tell those guys. If I see Hanrahan, I'm gonna kill him because I assume he's there to kill me.'

"We discussed the fact Kevin might go rogue. Pat said his entire face was purple, and he'd lost his glass eye during the fight. I'm not sure if it came out when he screamed 'my eye' or when the other guys gave him a beating in the street. After that, I concealed a long, slender bayonet everywhere I went. I still have it.

"As the story goes, Kevin soured on the Providence mob, feeling disrespected that he couldn't get even with me. That was the thing about guys back then, especially gangsters; it was all about respect. So, as I understand it, Kevin turned on Providence and began covertly working for the Boston faction, who were trying to take over. I heard Kevin got pinched trying to kidnap Blaise Marfeo outside the guy's restaurant. The arrest and a few other telltale incidents tipped the Providence mob off that Kevin had become a traitor.

"At River Café. Pat said to me, 'Remember that guy. He's not around anymore.'

"Which guy, Pat? There are a lot of guys."

"The hitter, Hanrahan," Pat said, making a gun with his fingers. "The one you gave a beating to."

Shortly after the incident, the doubts about Hanrahan's loyalty came to a head. He was shot and killed while walking on Federal Hill.

A former Mob member, Robert "Bobby" Deluca, now a government informant, pleaded guilty to conspiracy to kill Hanrahan. He named another well-known Mob associate as the shooter, but no one else has been charged.

Nothing more ever came of the problem between Hanrahan and Jimmy Vickers. Still, this delicate balance between alcohol-enhanced egos, mob guys and the wannabes, and the inevitable testosterone-fueled nightly violent clashes made for interesting times, as the Chinese curse goes.

*****

The wise guys weren't the only ones to raise problems within the club.

One Friday night, Gregg Moran and Chris Moran and their cousin stopped in. At closing, George was asking everyone to leave the club at closing time.

Pat remembers the incident this way.

"Gregg picked up a bar stool to hit George in the head; I was several feet away and grabbed the stool out of Gregg's hands

58

"Gregg, 6'3' 220lbs, and I got into a power struggle as I tried to run him out the back door; I get shoulder leverage and push him out to the hallway, then the other two guys jump on me, causing a free for all.

"My security comes into it, and we remove them out of the club. Gregg pulls out a 9 mm and waves it above his head. I found out later he was the brother of a Central Falls cop.

"The following Monday, I called and spoke to their brother, a Sergeant with Central Falls Police Department (CFPD), and he told me he would keep them out of the club."

About three weeks after the incident, a story appears on the news about the Moran brothers. They were arrested and charged with the robbery of a bar in CF.

The trio was convicted after trial, but the Supreme Court overturned the convictions. The following is from the Supreme Court decision.

"On April 27, 1992, two armed, masked men shattered the usual early

*morning quiet at Rick's Pub (Rick's) in
Central Falls when they burst into the
bar; ordered the manager, her
husband, and another pub employee to
the floor; and threatened to kill anyone
who looked at them. After rifling
through the cash register, they
absconded with less than $30. The
state later indicted Gregg Moran, his
brother, Chris, and their cousin,
George Gregoire (Gregoire), on a
myriad of criminal charges relating to
the robbery.[1] The state believed that
the Moran brothers were responsible
for the stickup at Rick's and that
Gregoire had driven the getaway car.
Trial, conviction, sentencing, and
appeal followed in due course.*

*The state's case began with the
testimony of Rick's manager, her
husband, and her assistant, all of
whom recited a grim but not unfamiliar
tale. On the morning of the crime two
masked marauders clad in black and*

wearing overcoats entered the pub. Brandishing guns and shouting instructions, they flung open the pub's door and ordered the three people present to hit the deck.   One of the thieves began barking, "Don't look at me!   Don't look at me or I'll kill ya!" Stunned, Rick's personnel fell silent and dropped to the floor while a robber vaulted over the bar, grabbed $30 from the cash register, and quickly egressed (with his sable sidekick in tow) without any valediction.

Because of the masks, no precise identification of the robbers was possible.   The best one of the witnesses could do was to describe the taller thief as being around six foot one and pudgy and the other one as being shorter, five foot nine or ten, but equally stout.   On cross-examination, however, the witness admitted telling the police that the robbers were slender and that the shorter one was only five foot six. (A police officer later testified that Gregg Moran is approximately six foot three, 220 pounds whereas Chris Moran is approximately six foot two, 190 pounds.)

Another witness (a Central Falls firefighter) picked up the story by telling the jury that he happened to be driving near Rick's when he saw two men quickly exit the building and jump into a white car. He called the police on his cellular phone and tailed the vehicle through the city streets until it parked behind a red Mustang or Capri. He said one of the men resembled Chris Moran. But he was never able to identify Chris Moran as one of the culprits.[2]

A later witness said that he also spied the gun-toting bandits as they hurriedly stormed into Rick's. He told the jury that he charged the getaway car and got a fleeting look at the driver's face. But the driver pulled out an automatic weapon (a KG-99 or a TEC-9) and threatened to blow him away. Understandably, the witness quickly retreated, and the car sped away. More importantly he failed to pick out Gregoire's photograph from two photo arrays, and he never identified him in court as the driver.

Armed with rough descriptions of these masked men and their getaway car, the police played a hunch and went to the home of Gregg Moran, their former colleague. There they found a red Capri with its engine still warm. They knocked on his apartment door and told him they wanted to talk. He refused to open the door. Tensions rose. One of the officers heard what he thought was the sound of a gun's being loaded.³ "Gregg, take it easy," another officer cajoled. "Calm down. Don't do anything stupid." Unmoved,

Moran replied that he would shoot anyone who crowded him, opened his door, or rushed into his apartment. He said that there was no way they were going to take him, adding that he would never go to prison.

About thirty minutes passed. Two additional Moran brothers (one of whom was a sergeant in the Central Falls police department), went to the scene. After hashing things out, Gregg said he would give himself up, but he wanted time to regroup. While waiting, the police heard a radio blaring, water running, cloth ripping, and a toilet flushing. Gregg then unlocked the door. Chris was with him. The police seized several weapons. Returning later that day with a search warrant, the police discovered, inter alia, a TEC-9 gun case, pieces of cloth stuffed inside the stovepipe and in the chimney, and rubber gloves in the Capri. (An officer

64

testified that Gregg used this type of glove while working as a mechanic.) Later, virtually on the eve of trial, the police found a TEC-9 gun in Gregg's new apartment.

A hair and fiber expert told the jury that tests showed that the clothes the Moran brothers were wearing when they surrendered had traces of material on them with the same microscopic properties as the pieces of cloth discovered in the chimney. He also said that the cloth pieces were consistent with materials used to make trench coats. Finally, a fingerprint expert linked two latent prints discovered on the exterior of the getaway car to Gregoire. It is significant that he could not say how long the prints had been on the car."

Based on several factors, the convictions were overturned. Later, they would enter a plea of guilty and receive a reduced sentence.

Colorful characters were a staple of the club scene, and episodes like this were not unique.

*****

The River Café was followed by a string of other clubs. Tilley Kings (Perrier's Nightclub), the former Corniche Nightclub called Tramp's, College Pub, and others. But one would put him squarely in the sights of Buddy's wrath, The Café Plaza.

In April 1990, Pat opened the Café Plaza. In what was once the comfort station in Kennedy Plaza, Pat transformed it into another successful business.

The following year, Buddy, having completed his deferred sentence from the DeLeo case (a minor incident where Buddy, with help from his police chauffeur, kidnapped and tortured Raymond DeLeo, a Bristol businessman who was having an affair with Buddy's wife, Sheila) and fresh off a successful run as the most popular WHJJ radio talk show host in Rhode Island, regained the office of mayor.

His office window overlooked Kennedy Plaza and Pat's business; whether this had anything to do with putting Pat on the Mayor's target list is anyone's guess. Still, it would be here that the relationship would strain and finally shatter.

In 1990, to keep himself in Cianci's good graces, Pat hosted a $1000 per ticket campaign fundraiser for Buddy at the Café Plaza location. While for the moment things seemed cordial, that was soon to change.

Café Plaza, Tilly Kings, and the Road to Confrontation

In 1990, Pat negotiated a $200,000 purchase and sales agreement with Solon Mitrelis of S & J 351 Inc. and took over the rest of a fifteen-year lease with the City of Providence for the former comfort station in Kennedy Plaza now operating as Café Plaza.

Pat made significant renovations, changing the name temporarily for six months, then reclaiming the site as Café Plaza.

For the first five years, things went well. The Café Plaza had an outside area for seating permitted by the Providence Parks Department.

All seemed fine.

Then the lease came up for renewal in 1995. In the original lease with S & J 351, the rent was set at four hundred dollars a month for the first five years, five hundred dollars and month for the second five years, and then negotiated for the next five years based on cost-of-living increases.

When Pat assumed the lease, he'd renegotiated a monthly rental of seven hundred fifty dollars plus two hundred fifty dollars for the patio. As part of the lease conditions, Pat was responsible for all maintenance and improvement costs, thus relieving the city of the burden. As the term of the lease expiration came closer, Pat contacted Cianci.

Standing in Cianci's office, Pat asked the mayor how to proceed.

"Go see Frank," Cianci said, giving Pat a wink of the eye.

Director of Administration Frank Corrente—who would later be indicted and convicted with Cianci during Operation Plunder Dome—handled negotiations for the city.

They didn't start well.

At trial in Superior Court, Pat recounted the meeting under questioning by his lawyer Geoffrey Regan.

"We sat in his office, and he took out the letter I had passed to him just then, and Corrente said, you can help us if we can help you."

"I said what do you mean by that?" Cortellessa testified.

He says, "do you own property on Eddy Street?"

I said, yes, I do. I had a piece of property on Eddy Street which was a restaurant at the time it was called Café Anzio

"What did Mr. Corrente say?" Regan asked. He said, "we want the business and the building too."

" Who is we?" Regan asked

"'He never elaborated," Cortellessa testified. 'I didn't ask.'

"'What happened next during the conversation?' Regan asked.

"I said that I couldn't help, I couldn't help him out because there was already a purchase and sales agreement' Cortellessa testified. 'He said,' you better break the agreement.'

I said, then I looked up at the ceiling, and I said, 'You know, Frank, your ceiling paint peeling you should have it painted.'

"What happened next during the conversation?' Regan asked.

"He got upset,' Cortellessa testified. 'I just wanted to leave the room disgusted with the fellow. He said, 'You better come back.' He waves the agreement. I never went back. Within a few days, Cortellessa testified he was told by the city Board of Licenses that the license allowing him to operate an outdoor patio at Café Plaza was revoked.

Leaving the office, Pat did not know what was coming. However, it would ultimately end up in front of the Supreme Court, where Pat's testimony regarding this unusual, if not unlawful, conversation was entered into the record over the city's objection.

The entire process descended into Armageddon between the city and Pat.

The negotiations dragged on into May 1995. Pat met with City Attorney Patricia McLaughlin and Parks Commissioner Nancy Derrig.

Derrig would later resign after an audit of the Parks Department uncovered large-scale theft of Parks Department funds by a subordinate.

Despite the binding clause that renegotiation of the lease be based on cost-of-living increases, the city wanted to raise the rent to three thousand dollars a month.

Negotiations reached a standstill. Pat, still operating under the belief Cianci was a friend called the mayor and asked him to "get these headhunters away from me."

When the city attorney involved in the negotiations found out about Pat contacting Cianci, she told him, "Stop dropping dimes to the mayor."

The effort to gain the mayor's help failed, so Pat was forced to seek relief in the courts. He operated under a Superior Court injunction for two years while the suit made its way through interrogatories, depositions, and court hearings.

Resigning himself to the inevitable, Pat's lawyer sent a letter to the city showing their willingness to accept the new lease cost.

In the letter, Pat's attorney, Geoffrey Regan, wrote, "...*While we do not concede the City has properly complied with its 'good faith negotiations' obligation to determine the amount of rent for the location under the fifteen-year option, we are mindful of the mounting costs of the litigation in this matter. Accordingly, I believe this matter is resolved and I would request you furnish this office with a copy of the new lease ready for signatures ready for my review."*

The response was not as expected. The city then began putting other conditions in place. They denied use of the outside patio and, at one point, said the location was selling too much coffee in the morning.

Pat was forced to take the case back to court to compel the city to negotiate in good faith. Pat got a stay on the termination of the lease while the case made its way through the courts.

Ultimately, the Rhode Island Supreme Court ruled 3-1 against Pat, and the case derailed.

The writing was on the wall. Pat's earlier rejection of an offer to buy Café Plaza for a concert venue by Mike Kent and Bob Bowen might have more to do with the negotiation failure than the rent price.

In a conversation with the mayor, he asked Pat what the holdup was with the Kent deal.

Pat said, "Kent has short pockets."

Mike Kent, a successful real estate developer and club owner, was a close associate of Buddy. Public records showed Kent purchased the carriage house on the mayor's former property on Power RD. for $200,000, thus helping the mayor avoid foreclosure.

Like many situations in dealing with Buddy Cianci, one could never be sure why things happened the way they did.

One thing was becoming clear, the mayor was not Cortellessa's friend and would support only those deals of benefit to his own interests.

Pat got a demolition permit, knocked down most of the building improvements, removed the equipment, and walked away. When a furious Cianci found out about the damage to the building, he sent the Providence Police to investigate. But, with the demo permit on file, there was little the city could do.

The city's unwillingness to negotiate in good faith—whatever the motivation—accomplished nothing. Rather than a vibrant business at the location, the city had an empty building. Moreover, the maintenance of the vacant building now fell to the city—no income, no business, no improvements, decaying property—for four years.

This confrontation was a long-time in the making. Pat now understood this through the benefit of hindsight. On reflection, he now saw the earlier signs of trouble.

The stage for the showdown with the mayor was set back when Pat purchased a building at 525 Eddy Street. The building once housed a club called Tilly Kings then Vertigo, but Vertigo was failing.

The owner of Tilly King's, John "Tilly King" Gomes, went missing on November 21, 1984. His body was found in the woods of Rt. 195 in Westport, MA. No one has been charged with his murder, but police suspect it was mob-related.

According to news reports on May 21, 2021, Massachusetts authorities are exploring a connection between the late Kevin Hanrahan, a notorious mob enforcer who was himself a victim of a mob hit, and Gomes' murder.

According to Bristol County District Attorney Thomas Quinn, investigators are still pursuing suspects, including Hanrahan.

> *"But there was no corroborative evidence that would have led to charges [at the time]," Quinn said. "The conduct would not be inconsistent with what he's done in the past, so we have information that he's linked to it, and we're going to review the case." (WPRI 12, 2021)*

It was with this backdrop Pat bought the building, and his troubles with the mayor began.

Forming PCRL Realty, Pat bought the building and the business, taking ownership of the liquor license and all related business licenses.

The club went through various iterations until it reopened as 1st Impressions, an adult entertainment club.

This drew the likes of Charles Sonny Keeler, who was involved with several adult clubs, Rocco Argenti, a member of the Providence Mob, Carl Ferraro, now deceased and the founder of the Providence Chapter of the Hell's Angels, serving as President.

Several Providence Police officers, among them Nick Ricamo, a close friend of Chuck Keeler, also had connections to the club.

With a long history of managing such clubs, Keeler believed the owners were not running the place the right way. After trying to straighten out the operation left to work at Cheaters, another strip club.

Clubs such as these, with high cash flow, always drew the attention of the mob. At one point, Frank Salemme Jr., son of reputed mob boss Frank "Cadillac Frank" Salemme, Sr., tried to extort money for protection from the club. Rocco Argenti, using his influence with the Providence mob, blocked the attempt.

Such is often the price of doing business in this world. Soon, the neighbors complained about problems outside the club, and the police brought complaints about the disturbances inside the club.

The trouble peaked with the murder of a bouncer in front of the club. Accusations were made the killing was an attempt to force the club owners to pull out. Still, ultimately the shooting happened because of an earlier fight that resulted in the shooter being kicked out of the club.

He returned with a gun and shot the bouncer.

Pat decided it was time to change it up, get rid of the current club owners, and renovate. So in October 1994, he reopened it as Café Anzio, an Italian Restaurant.

The restaurant lasted a year, and Pat decided it was time to sell the business but hang on to the building.

Under the city provisions, prior use of the location, which included adult entertainment, made the sale more attractive to potential buyers.

Putting the word out that the business and licenses were for sale, Pat got inquiries from many people, some with previous connections to 1st Impressions and some new faces.

Bobby Walason, a formidable member of the Bobo Marrapese crew, and his partner Sonny Montrond met with Pat. Walason and Pat knew each other from Walason's time working as security at the Gallery and his connections with Bobo.

After a brief meeting, they decided not to buy the place.

Sonny Keeler and Nick Ricamo, the Providence Police officer with close connections to Buddy Cianci, took a look at it but also walked away.

Even Rocco Argenti, another feared Mob associate, made an offer to buy. But, unfortunately, he had no money and wanted Pat to fund a loan, so the negotiations went nowhere. Knowing such deals ended in one of two ways—neither of which involved getting the loan repaid—Pat declined.

Enter into the picture Frank Viola, a Boston banker and President of Haymarket Bank in Boston, and William Deyesso, a Boston business executive who owned several adult entertainment clubs.

This group had the experience and financial wherewithal to make the business successful and, most importantly, the money to buy the business from Pat and run a club that paid its rent.

Once again, the inner workings of the City of Providence reared their ugly head. Preparing the paperwork for the license transfers, Pat had to secure a signature from Ramzi Loqa, Director of the Department of Inspection and Standards for the city, who had signed off on the original use permits.

Loqa refused to sign the permit, claiming he did not recall the original use or that the location had once operated as an adult entertainment venue. Despite having signed the permits for two years while 1st Impressions was in operation and providing the permits to the Board of Licenses, which approved the Adult Entertainment License for the location.

Without his signature, the deal was dead in the water. The implication was simple: somebody in the city did not want an outside business entity to get the location.

And this is where a little of the only in Rhode Island and the Cianci influence combine to turn things around.

Buddy Cianci was friendly with a particular doctor. As luck would have it, Frank Viola also knew the same doctor and mentioned the problems he was having getting the deal for the building to go through.

And just like that, the problem was solved. Within days, Pat had Loqa's signature on the use permits, the Zoning Board signed off, the transfer of the licenses was approved, and Providence had its newest strip club, Centerfolds.

This would not be the only connection to Buddy intertwined in this deal.

William Deyesso, Viola's partner in the business, was arrested in June 1996 after he returned from Russia with $27,000 at Logan International Airport in Boston. In October 1996, he pleaded guilty to two felony counts, including failure to file reports on the export and import of monetary instruments. He was ordered to forfeit $26,979 and was fined $10,000. He also was placed on probation for three years and ordered to perform 150 hours of community service.

In 1997, Frank Viola transferred his interest in the business to Richard McCabe, who became partners with Deyesso in Centerfolds.

In 1988, McCabe bought another adult venue in Worcester, called Pudgy's, from Peter Devito. Pudgy's became the Worcester Centerfolds, and Devito went to work for McCabe managing the Centerfolds in Providence.

Ellen Brogna, the wife of former Winter Hill gang leader Howie Winter, claimed she was cheated because she owned fifty-two percent of Pudgy's, even though Devito was listed as the owner. She claimed Devito owned just 15 percent.

Whatever the truth behind the ownership mattered little. In December 2001, Devito was inside the Squire Lounge, a strip joint in Revere, MA. A gunman walked up to Devito, called his name, and shot him three times at close range.

In 2005, a notorious mob enforcer, Billy "The Angel" Angelesco, was charged with Devito's murder. He was acquitted after trial. The motive behind Devito's murder was never clear, but this was during a major power struggle within the Patriarca family. Fierce competition between Boston and Connecticut factions led to some killings.

The strip club business, a goldmine for cash, was an easy target for extortion payments. With these overtones, Cianci dabbled by inserting himself into licensing problems and accepting money from the business owners.

During Buddy's final—and failed—run for office, Deyesso made two $500 donations to the campaign. This showed the relationship was a long-term one, not a one-off situation.

Following questions from a Providence Journal reporter, Cianci said he would return the Deyesso donation, trying to distance himself from the story.

In the Journal article, Cianci said,

"I have never heard of William Deyesso, but based on the information you provided us regarding his background, I will return his donation immediately."

Many corporation stockholders that ran the club were frequent, generous contributors to Cianci's campaign fund, as listed on the Mayor's Campaign Finance Reports.

Just another of the many coincidences linked to the former mayor and the inner workings of the city.

It would be these issues—the delay in transferring licenses, losing Café Plaza, costing Pat's company a loss of over $250000—that would spur Pat to run for office against Buddy and work to eliminate this aura of corruption and backroom dealing.

In 2000, the Rhode Island Department of Transportation bought the building for the 195-relocation project. As a result, Centerfolds was forced to close, unable to find a suitable location to operate.

It was the end of one story, but not the end of *the* story of the war brewing between Pat and Buddy.

Pat playing football at Central High

Pat returns to his Alma Mater

Pat with Roland Lemonthe at the Gallery

Pat working the door at 21 East

Dance! Twenty One East

DJ George from 21 East and Jo-Ann White

Slade's Pub

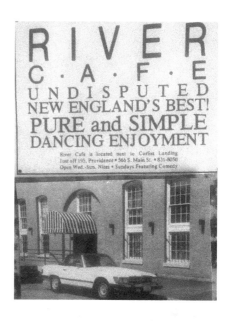

Buddy cutting the ribbon a River Cafe

Pat at Slades Pub

Pat and DJ George

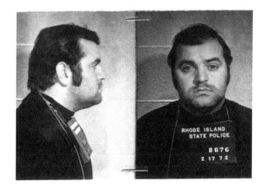

```
R.I. State Police Ident. No. 8676
Name      Marrapese, Frank Louigi
Alias     "Bobo"
```

RISP Arrest Photo Frank "Bobo" Marrapese

Happier times at Café Plaza

Peter and Bonnie Wilkins Owners 21 East

Vacant lot Pat wanted to turn into a restaurant. Unfortunately, the land sat unused for years.

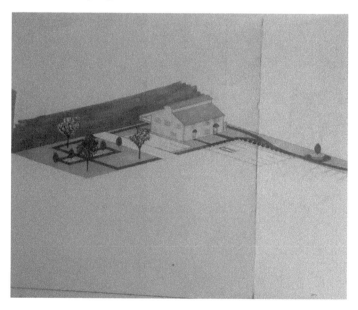

Pat's vision for the vacant lot

State of Rhode Island and Providence Plantations

SENATOR
JOHN M. RONEY
344 Wickenden Street
Providence, Rhode Island 02903

Room 21, State House
Providence, Rhode Island 02903

401-421-9794
Fax: 401-421-0132

Committee on Finance

Committee on Special Legislation

Vice Chairman,
Joint Committee on Environment
and Energy

Senate Chamber

July 26, 1995

Councilman John J. Lombardi
Chairman of Committee on City Properties
City Hall
25 Dorrance Street
Providence, RI 02903

Dear Chairman Lombardi:

In the past we have opposed large scale development projects in the Corliss Landing/India Point waterfront area because of potential traffic overflow into the Fox Point residential neighborhood. This does not mean, however, that we would oppose all development plans for this area particularly those on a smaller scale.

With this in mind, we support Patrick Cortellessa's proposal for a 75-person waterfront restaurant at 668 South Water Street. This small scale development would enhance the waterfront area and add significantly to the City's tax revenue without adversely affecting the existing social and traffic problems. This restaurant project will attract an older crowd and will give important balance to the area.

Therefore, assuming that the legitimate concerns of the area residents and business owners are addressed satisfactorily, we support Mr. Cortellessa's restaurant development plan.

Senator John M. Roney

JMR:js:senate\cortell.ltr

Rep. Paul E. Moura

Old Harbor Marina and Pat's plan for development torpedoed by Buddy

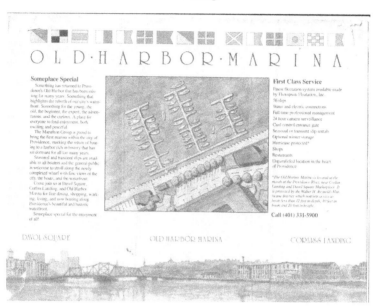

OLD·HARBOR·MARINA

Someplace Special

Something has returned to Providence's Old Harbor that has been missing for many years. Something that highlights the rebirth of our city's waterfront. Something for the young, the old, the beginner, the expert, the adventurous, and the curious. A place for everyone to find enjoyment, both exciting and peaceful.

The Marathon Group is proud to bring the first marina within the city of Providence, marking the return of boating to a harbor rich in history that has sat dormant for all too many years.

Seasonal and transient slips are available to all boaters and the general public is welcome to stroll along the newly completed wharf with fine views of the city, the boats, and the waterfront.

Come join us at Davol Square, Corliss Landing, and Old Harbor Marina for fine dining, shopping, working, living, and new boating along Providence's beautiful and historic waterfront.

Someplace special for the enjoyment of all!

First Class Service

Finest flotation system available made by Flotation, Inc.
56 slips
Water and electric connections
Full time professional management
24 hour camera surveillance
Card control entrance gate
Seasonal or transient slip rentals
Optional winter storage
Hurricane protected*
Shops
Restaurants
Unparalleled location in the heart of Providence

The Old Harbor Marina is located at the mouth of the Providence River, near Corliss Landing and Davol Square Marketplace. It is protected by the Walter H. Reynolds Hurricane Barrier which restricts access to boats less than 12 feet in depth, 10 feet in beam and 20 feet in height.

Call (401) 331-5900

DAVOL SQUARE   OLD HARBOR MARINA   CORLISS LANDING

Artist rendition of Old Harbor Marina Plans

Return of the King

In 1990, Buddy won re-election to the Office of Mayor. Promising a new start, he returned to his role as a popular candidate despite never having received even close to a majority of votes cast.

That's the thing about Providence Mayoral races, the candidate with the *most* votes wins. Thus Buddy, elected and re-elected to the office more than any other candidate, had more people vote against him than for him.

And yet, here he was, back in the mayor's office once again.

The conflict with Pat soon began with Café Plaza and escalated from there. Frank Corrente, Cianci's frontman and Director of Administration, handled the day-to-day operations, but, as the RICO case later established, nothing happened in the City with the Mayor having a hand in it.

While the stage had been set for confrontation, Buddy was operating with caution. Aware the U.S.

Attorney's Office might be keeping an eye on things, Cianci focused on projects to improve the city.

In 1994, the culmination of the Providence River Relocation Project was highlighted by the first lighting of *Waterfire*, the award-winning river-based project by Barnaby Evans. The project showcased the now uncovered river and won national awards for creativity.

Cianci would often float in a gondola along the river, a glass of wine in hand, reveling in the enthusiastic crowds of tourists and residents enjoying the spectacle.

For those unaware of the inner workings of the Cianci administration, the city seemed poised to rise to new levels of success. The saddest part of this story is that the city's renaissance was real, and Buddy played a role. Even if that role was more cheerleader than the primary force behind the success, he was an enthusiastic cheerleader.

The reality is multiple factors were contributing to the rise of Providence on the national stage. Buddy was loath to acknowledge such outside influences, but the renaissance was real.

Others would soon learn a darker side was also poised to emerge and engulf the success in a wave of corruption and indictments.

Pat had a way to get into the mayor's office and met with Buddy to discuss various development plans. The mayor often seemed enthusiastic and supportive.

Pat bought a building at 56-70 Washington Street and ran the former Anthony's Restaurant and later called it Skipper's Pub. He opened several more locations; one was the Ambassador Club, all with splendid success.

As a matter of business relations, Pat attended many of Cianci's fundraisers—at $500 a ticket—and the relationship seemed solid.

But that was all to change.

A Vacant Lot and a Sweetheart Deal

In 1987, Pat's River Café was humming along. But, unfortunately, the proximity to Roosters—just one block away—DJ George moving to Pat's place, and Pat's success with the club contributed to the animosity among some club owners.

Nearby was a vacant lot of land at 465 South Water Street, owned by the city. Since it was empty, the city received no property taxes on the land.

By May 1987, Rooster's nightclub building was knocked down. The original plans called for building condos. Instead, running into financial issues with the original plan, the developers bought a franchise. Investing significant money, the building eventually became Shooter's Nightclub.

But before this took place, the owners of Rooster's signed a Purchase and Sales agreement to buy and tow two barges from New York and hauled them onto the now vacant land.

The then Mayor, Joe Paolino Jr., denied the owner use of the property, and the barges were abandoned, left to rust and decay on the property where they remained for some time.

One afternoon, the owner of Roosters and Anthony St. Laurent, a capo in the Patriarca Mob family, came into the River Café looking for Pat's help in persuading Mayor Paolino to agree to the lease of the land.

Pat declined. It would not be the last effort by others to lease the land from the city.

In 1995, Mike Kent, a close associate of Buddy Cianci, asked the city to lease the land for an outdoor concert venue.

The neighbors objected, and the plan was denied.

Pat, always one to seize an opportunity, approached the city about leasing the property and building a restaurant up on stilts.

He offered the city $40,000 in annual payments on a fifteen-year lease. If the city accepted the offer, they would net over $600,000 in tax revenue from property that had been abandoned for all intent and purposes.

Meeting with John Lombardi, the President of the City Council and chairperson of the Providence Property committee, Pat got a tentative agreement for the plan.

Lombardi recommended Pat get a letter of support from the local representatives to assuage any neighborhood concerns. Reaching out, Pat got a letter supporting the project from then-Representative Paul Moura and the late Providence Senator John Roney endorsing the proposal.

Letter in hand, Pat delivered a copy to the Providence Property committee and a copy to the mayor's office.

Cianci then objected to the agreement and derailed further discussions for the lease. Allegedly Cianci was not happy about the letters supporting the project.

Just another example of backroom shenanigans with Buddy et al.

By this time, 1992-1995, Pat had learned to deal with the ins and outs of the Cianci world. He continued to finance businesses, Cactus Grill (the old location of the River Café) and Jazz Express at 580 South Main. Making each one a success.

Ambassador Restaurant and the Setup

In 1997, Providence Police complained to the Board of Licenses alleging drug dealing was taking place inside the Ambassador, Pat's club at 78 Washington Street.

When Pat and his attorney appeared before the License board, the police witness, Anthony Greenwood, testified he was pressured by Providence Police to claim drugs were being sold in the club and that he bought them inside.

On the stand, he said after speaking to his priest, he couldn't lie.

The hearing was stopped, and the board went into a closed session. After a few moments, they called Pat in. The panel offered a 10-day voluntary suspension to address all the complaints. There would be no acknowledgment of any drug dealing.

Pat weighed his options. He could continue to fight the suspension, costing him time, money, and lost business, or cut his losses and close for ten-day.

He opted to close.

But he knew Buddy would not be happy with the result and would be watching the place for strict compliance.

Unable to resist, Pat thumbed his nose at the mayor while still complying with the closure. Knowing the Mayor would, on his nightly crawl through the city checking on his friends and enemies, drive by, Pat left the neon lights on in the window.

One night in the middle of the suspension, Pat received a call from Ray Dettore, chairperson of the Board of Licenses, demanding he close the business. Pat chuckled at the request.

"Just tell the mayor the business is closed; nobody said anything about leaving the lights off."

Whether or not this infuriated the mayor is anyone's guess. Still, the confrontation now set in motion was not soon to end. Pat still tried to maintain a cordial, if not friendly, relationship but the first signs of fraying had begun.

Waterfront Plans: The Old Harbor Marina

In 1992, Pat met with the landlord of The Old Harbor Marina, Arnold Kilberg. Pat proposed leasing the building for a restaurant and pub.

An agreement was reached, and Pat commissioned blueprints for the renovations. Because the building had been built with Providence Redevelopment Agency (PRA) funds, the city had to approve the change of use for the building.

Pat arranged a meeting with the mayor.

Walking into the Mayor's office on a bright, sunny afternoon, Buddy greeted Pat like an old friend. He looked over the plans and pronounced them excellent.

"Let's get this done, Pat," Buddy said. "This will be great for the waterfront."

Reaching for the phone, he summoned Frank Corrente, his Director of Administration, to the office.

Corrente looked over the plans, agreed they were excellent, and told the mayor he would get the thing moving right away.

Pat left the office confidant he had the mayor's blessing, and the review by the PRA would be a formality.

A month later, Pat had the approval from the licensing board for a Class BX Liquor License. Things seemed to go as the Mayor and Corrente promised.

Then, Pat got a call from Kilberg. The mayor wanted to hold up the project for a few months. There were rumblings in the neighborhood concerned over more traffic with the addition of another bar/restaurant.

Such things are often encountered in the business world, so Pat was unfazed. Instead, he deferred the work and said he would hold off for three months to let the situation quiet down.

Two months passed, and Pat contacted Kilberg to get the keys and schedule the renovations. But, unfortunately, it was then the Mayor's Machiavellian personality showed itself once again.

Kilberg told Pat the Mayor wanted someone else to take over the property, telling Kilberg to let Pat know he "owed him a big favor."

As is often the case in Rhode Island, the story of Arnold Kilberg had ties to the Patriarca family. Ostensibly these were legitimate ties, but they existed nevertheless.

Kilberg made his money as a broker licensed by the U.S. Small Business Administration to lend taxpayer money to small businesses.

The Chicago Tribune wrote an extensive article about the business dealings of Arnold Kilberg.

> *"Under the SBA program, Kilberg was supposed to borrow the money from the SBA at, say, 8 percent and relend it to disadvantaged Americans at a higher interest rate, say 15 percent. The program allows Kilberg's firms to pocket the difference between what he pays to the government and what he charges the borrower once his costs are deducted. He also charges borrowers fees on the loans.*

109

Kilberg has had no trouble finding borrowers, although many of his loans should have raised questions with SBA officials charged with oversight of the federal program.

In 1990, for example, one of his companies arranged for a $1.7 million loan to a Virgin Islands hotel company whose president, Kilberg's former neighbor Benedetto A. Cerilli Jr., currently faces criminal racketeering charges for alleged misuse of an investment bank.

In 1991, one of Kilberg's companies also lent $3.1 million to a Rhode Island shipyard whose president, Kreso Bezmalinovic, had three years earlier pleaded guilty to paying an illegal gratuity to a federal Environmental Protection Agency inspector, in a case involving a New

York asbestos removal company he ran.

The same year his companies lent $5 million to the Rocky Point Amusement Park, a 155-year-old facility in Warwick, R.I., treasured by New Englanders for its corkscrew roller coaster ride and clam-cake dining hall. One of its owners, Boston real estate and nightclub magnate Henry D. Vara Jr., had some troubles, too.

In 1989, the Nevada Gaming Commission granted a Massachusetts-based company the right to buy the Sands Hotel for $127 million on the condition that its investors cut their business ties to Vara. An official said drugs were sold out of Vara's nightclubs, and profits were being skimmed.

At the time, Massachusetts Gov. Michael Dukakis told several state lawmakers that his administration would not "do business with Mr. Vara," according to a suit Vara filed in a Massachusetts county court.

Vara, whose investment portfolio included Florida television stations and a Colorado youth prison, filed court papers saying he was not associated with organized crime and was being treated unfairly because of his Italian heritage.

Vara was not Kilberg's only questionable client. In 1987, Kilberg put together a $750,000 loan for a real estate firm ostensibly headed by the wife of reputed New England crime syndicate boss Raymond Patriarca Jr. The loan was paid off, but an SBA auditor cited Kilberg's firm for minor infractions. In 1991, Patriarca pleaded guilty to extortion, drug trafficking and gambling and is now serving a 10-year federal prison term.

The other loans had bigger troubles. The Virgin Islands resort defaulted on its $1.7 million loan, and Kilberg's brokerage took an ownership stake in the hotel. The shipyard filed for bankruptcy last August, and the loan to the amusement park went unpaid. Rocky Point filed for bankruptcy in 1994.

Despite the fiascos, Kilberg lives well. According to some 1994 court records, he drew personal income of more than $450,000 a year from the brokerages, his accounting firm and about $6 million worth of Rhode Island properties.

One of the reasons he seems to prosper despite the bad loans is his ability to make money servicing the borrowers through his network of interrelated companies. Kilberg's accounting firm has helped prepare financial records for companies that have borrowed from his SBA-backed brokerage, court records show.

Kilberg comes along after a deal encounters trouble and picks up the pieces. Once the Rocky Point amusement park went under, for instance, an attorney for the park's unsecured creditors filed court papers accusing the owners of having skimmed profits--a charge they denied. Under a reorganization plan, a new corporation controlled by Kilberg was created to manage the carnival, court records show.

Local citizens groups fought in court to save the historic park, but Kilberg's company was given court permission to auction off the rides to pay delinquent taxes and now plans to subdivide the property and sell it to real estate developers.

To preserve access to the historic shoreline, state and local officials are

114

currently negotiating to pay Kilberg's company as much as $3 million to buy a strip of it.

All of this, of course, hasn't gone unnoticed by the government. The SBA approved the payments to his accounting firm.

In 1993, an SBA official notified one of Kilberg's partners that because of "significant regulatory violations," the SBA was willing to permit two of the loan companies to continue operating "only on the condition that Mr. Arnold Kilberg is removed from positions of management."

A report this April report by the General Accounting Office cited Kilberg's dealings as an example of how the SBA's lax oversight had allowed the program to be marked by waste and fraud.

Nevertheless, Kilberg is still operating. He is not a man without influence.

State Republican Party chief Holmes, who is an investment adviser, has rented office space from Kilberg, and steered cash-strapped small businesses to him, records and interviews show.

In February 1992, Holmes Financial Services even took out a full-page ad in the Providence Business News. Captioned, "Where to go when the bank says no," the ad listed a dozen businesses that had been financed through Holmes by Kilberg's government-backed loan companies.

Today, only three of those loans are performing smoothly. Six of the companies, with a total of more than $12 million in loans, filed for bankruptcy. Three others, with loans totaling $2.6 million, are seriously *delinquent,   court   records   and interviews show." (Jackson, 1996)*

Thus, the agreement for Pat to build a restaurant fell apart, and a new group emerged. The new people were the owners of Shooters and, coincidentally, where the mayor docked his boat.

All these machinations over licensing issues, lease agreements, broken promises all ran simultaneously with Pat's growing realization that the mayor, and the way he ran the city, were focused on just one thing. And it was not Pat's success unless it had a direct benefit to Buddy.

In 1996, the trial over the Café Plaza took place in Superior Court before Judge Thomas Needham. Pat lost, and Needham ruled for the city.

By this time, Pat had posted signs for his first run for Mayor. It was a more defensive move than an actual political challenge, but that would soon change.

While the appeal was pending before the Supreme Court, Buddy walked into the Café Plaza to speak to Pat. They moved to an outside table away from everyone.

Buddy paused for a moment, then said something that caught Pat off-guard.

"You know if you want to stay here, you have to run as a Republican. People think I put you up to running for Mayor just to increase donations for my campaign; I could make some money on it."

The implication was clear to Pat. Play along, and he could have his lease. He answered by saying, "Don't try to make me a politician."

Cianci stood abruptly and walked away. Later, when Pat had time to think, he realized he should have just agreed to the mayor's idea, and things might have turned out better.

Pat had a campaign headquarters in his building on Washington Street. Inside were the assets of the Turks Club Pat had purchased, giving the offices an impressive looking ambiance.

Frank Corrente walked by and opened the door.

"Hey," Corrente said, "do those phones really work? You having fun?"

Pat said, "I'm having a great time. Things are going great."

The campaign went from a lark to the real thing. Pat now faced the biggest challenge of Providence, taking on the mayor on the political stage.

If doing business was complicated and fraught with pitfall, running against Cianci was full-blown combat with no rules of engagement.

Into the Dragon's Lair

Challenging Buddy Cianci at the Polls

"But a lie is a lie, and in itself intrinsically evil, whether it be told with good or bad intents." ~

Immanuel Kant

Mayoral Campaign 1997-1998:
Baptism by Fire

In 1997, on a TV show called *Rhode Island Gathers*, Pat Cortellessa faced Buddy Cianci in a debate. Raising the issues of unfunded pension liabilities, deals over unaffordable Cost-of-Living Adjustments (COLAs), and a poor small business environment, Cortellessa demanded the mayor provide answers.

Cianci retorted with the failed Café Plaza site as an example of Pat's poor business record, conveniently forgetting the city itself, under the command of Cianci himself, forced Pat out.

Then he raised Centerfolds as an example of Pat bringing the wrong businesses into the city. Once again, ignoring the part he played in expediting the adult entertainment and liquor license transfer, plus accepting campaign contributions from stockholders in Centerfolds.

To say it was a less than cordial debate is an understatement. But this was just the opening volley.

The main action would be brutal, clearly demonstrating the lengths to which the mayor would go not to just defeat his opponents but to obliterate them.

Former Attorney General Arlene Violet turned popular radio talk show host quipped about the events leading to Pat's removal from the ballot that "Cianci used a howitzer to kill a mouse."

But the details of the events leading to Pat's disqualification are even more troubling.

Ballot Signatures and Intimidation

To run for Mayor, one has to obtain at least five hundred signatures from registered voters. So Pat's supporters fanned out into the neighborhoods seeking support.

When they were done, the campaign submitted eight hundred and two. The Board of Canvassers certified five hundred thirty-four, and Pat is on the ballot.

Not so fast.

The political machine does not care for competition. So the city Democratic Party filed a challenge alleging fraud in the nomination papers.

Cianci sent city workers, accompanied by Providence Police officers, to interview anyone who signed the papers.

Fifteen of those interviewed signed affidavits that they did not sign the nomination papers. Whether intimidation or threats played a part is anyone's guess. However, even with removing these signatures,

Pat still qualified for the election with five hundred nineteen.

Once again, not so fast.

The Board of Canvassers held a special hearing. In the initial moments, a lawyer representing the local Democratic Party urged the board to disqualify Cortellessa as a candidate and ask Police Chief Urbano Prignano to open a criminal investigation.

Referring to the fifteen affidavits presented to the board, the lawyer claimed the Cortellessa campaign engaged in "a pattern of rampant fraud, forgery, and felonious conduct."

The backdrop to these allegations could not have been any clearer. The Providence Journal, in a story about the hearing from July 23, 1998, Metro Edition by C. J. Chivers reported,

> *"It was also an unmistakable statement of City Hall power.*
>
> *Five police officers, including two detectives and one of Cianci's former limousine drivers, stood along the wall. Artin H. Coloian, the mayor's executive*

help, moved throughout the room, trying unsuccessfully to control a smile."

The message was evident to Cortellessa supporters. If you challenge the king, you will face the full power of the throne. You cannot wound a tyrant; you must destroy him.

The Democrats, clearly supporting Cianci, went for Pat's jugular. They went after his candidacy on two fronts, claiming fraud and forgery on the nomination papers and that Cortellessa was not a Providence resident.

As they pressed their case, they asked to withdraw the residency issue and focus on what they saw as their most potent play.

Claiming they anticipated having more affidavits by the end of the day, which would drive the total below the necessary five hundred signatures, they urged the board to disqualify Pat from the ballot.

Jack Potter, himself a Democratic candidate for Governor in 1998, rose to defend Pat.

From the same Providence Journal article,

"Even with the somber police present, the crowd grew restless. Potter stood and demanded that the federal authorities look into the Board of Canvassers.

'This is an attempt to railroad Mr. Cortellessa, he said, and swept his hand toward Quinlan and Mancini. 'If anyone is fraudulent here, maybe that's the two fellas.'

He also accused the party and board of executing a setup. Standing near the table and raising his voice, Potter testified that he had signed Cortellessa's papers himself, only to have Mancini's staff members call him and try to coerce him to say otherwise—under a threat of a perjury charge...

The article ends with this last comment by Potter.

"'Everything,' Potter said, 'pointed to Cianci, and he had had enough.

'Now you can see why no one runs
against the son-of-a-bitch.'"

Despite testimony to the contrary, the signs of intimidation and threats, and that some signatures were unchallenged, the board removed two full pages of signatures from Pat's nomination papers.

His total of valid signatures dropped below the five hundred needed to be listed on the ballot.

The only serious challenger to Cianci's re-election, one who would force Cianci to spend his precious campaign funds warding off the challenge, was now gone.

Fast forward to another election in 2018 for City Council. Again, one candidate moved to have an entire page of signatures removed from his opponent's nomination papers even though only one signature was invalid.

In support of his motion, he cited Cianci vs. Cortellessa as precedent. However, the State Board of Elections ruled only the invalid signature needed to be removed.

Thus, had the State Board intervened in the Cianci vs. Cortellessa matter, the mayoral election of 1998 would have been quite different.

But despite Cianci's return to office, the first rumbles of the coming apocalypse that would tear the city asunder were just over the horizon.

As a backdrop to the public political machinations of the Cianci machine attacking Pat's candidacy, another, less public, drama was unfolding.

In April 1996, Pat was interviewed by the FBI regarding the circumstances around his Café Plaza business and the events surrounding Pat's involvement.

During the interview with the FBI, Pat told the agents the entire story behind his efforts to place a Dunkin' Donuts franchise at the Café Plaza location.

This is the report from the FBI obtained through the Freedom of Information Act.

In or around 1991 CORTELLESSA wanted to put a Dunkin donut franchise in the cafe Plaza building at

129

Kennedy Plaza CORTELLESSA ran the idea past Mayor VINCENT CIANCI who gave close a verbal OK to pursue the Dunkin' Donuts franchise

"CORTELLESSA was subsequently contacted by Providence businessman [NAME REDACTED] who told CORTELLESSA that he was interested in buying the cafe Plaza and putting in a [redacted information] franchise for that location

CORTELLESSA subsequently met with [NAME REDACTED] was the individual who was going to put the franchise in the Cafe Plaza if [NAME REDACTED] purchased the business from CORTELLESSA

In a meeting that occurred between CORTELLESSA and [NAME REDACTED] this person was told CORTELLESSA he did not like putting money in paper bags and stated that he would handle that end

130

CORTELLESSA understood this to mean that the cash payoff would have to be made to public officials in order to facilitate the franchise being allowed in Kennedy Plaza

[NAME REDACTED] subsequently offered CORTELLESSA approximately 100 and $25,000 for the cafe Plaza business in court also turned him down

No Dunkin' Donuts franchise will ever put in the cafe Plaza building.

CORTELLESSA has heard several bits of information on the street relative to former Cianci aide [NAME REDACTED] was building a house in [information redacted]

CORTELLESSA has heard that workers from the [information redacted] construction company worked on the house while they were supposed to be doing work on the construction of the Fleet Skating center

In addition, CORTELLESSA has heard several rumors relative to an illegal or questionable sewer hookup at [location redacted] a new residence while at [location redacted] construction site CORTELLESSA saw a dumpster which he believed to be owned by a city vendor.

CORTELLESSA supplied photocopies of documents relative to the Dunkin' Donuts Cafe Plaza issue as well as the failure of the city to renew his lease at the Cafe Plaza in 1995 the details which were previously furnished by CORTELLESSA in his April 1996 interview contained in FBI reference 9194C -PS 71217 serial 197.

(FBI Freedom of Information Act (FOIA) Request re: Cortellessa FOI/ PA# 1457756-0)

Pat was aware relaying such information to the FBI might trigger an investigation. He also knew lying to the FBI was a felony and needed to tread lightly as a businessperson. Still, he also knew he did not want to be part of the corruption necessary to deal with some members of the Cianci administration.

What he didn't know at the time was an enterprising FBI agent named Dennis Aiken had set his sights on the mayor and his administration. Assisted by the Rhode Island State Police, the FBI was about to cast a wide net around the city.

Plunder Dome:

The Decline and Fall of Buddy Cianci

"No man is an island,

Entire of itself.

Each is a piece of the continent,

A part of the main.

If a clod be washed away by the

sea,

Europe is the less.

As well as if a promontory were.

As well as if a manor of thine

own

Or of thine friend's were.

Each man's death diminishes me,

For I am involved in mankind.

Therefore, send not to know

For whom the bell tolls,

It tolls for thee."

For Whom the Bell Tolls, John Donne

Death Knell for a Political Career

In the summer of 1997, while Cianci's campaign gyrations and political chicanery vs. Cortellessa played out before the Providence Board of Canvassers, another panel met secretly in the federal courthouse.

An investigation—code-named Plunder Dome— was underway, with mountains of evidence presented to a federal grand jury.

The genesis of the case was questionable lease agreements between the city and Edward Voccola, a property owner and convicted felon.

Several city officials were called to testify under oath before the grand jury. Under federal law, matters before the grand jury are secret. Witnesses are admonished not to disclose their testimony or subject of any questioning.

It strains credulity that city employees appointed by the mayor would abide by such restrictions. Still, we can only surmise the mayor knew about the proceedings.

The case focused on Frank Corrente, Cianci's long-time Director of Administration. He had played a significant role in securing the leases by the school department for Voccola.

In January 1998, the FBI received information from a local business owner, Antonio Freitas, that his lower qualifying bids for the leases were rejected in favor of Voccola.

Alleging there was a "pay to play" scheme to inflate the bids and pay bribes, Freitas agreed to wear a wire.

During the ensuing months, Freitas would meet with Joe Pannone, chairman of the Providence Board of Tax Assessment Review, and record hundreds of conversations and bribery payments.

On April 28, 1999, the first public indication of something amiss at city hall hit the media.

FBI agents and state police executed search warrants at city hall, seizing records from five offices. The apocalypse was upon the mayor, and he went into full defensive mode.

Denying any wrongdoing, Cianci claimed any actions by those in his administration, if illegal, were done without his knowledge. He defended Corrente and Pannone, claiming it was a witch hunt by overzealous federal prosecutors.

In May 1999, Joseph Pannone was indicted on ten corruption charges.

Three counts of conspiracy, three counts of attempted extortion, three counts of mail fraud, and one count of money laundering.

Rosemary Glancy, the deputy city tax collector, was charged with seven counts in the same indictment. Two counts of conspiracy, two counts of attempted extortion, and three counts of money laundering.

In December 1999, Pannone pleaded guilty to fourteen charges related to conspiracy to commit extortion, attempted extortion, and mail fraud. The charges of money laundering were dismissed.

Pannone agreed to cooperate with the government in the ongoing investigation.

From the FBI files on the investigation,

"This plea may have far-reaching effects in view of the extensive statement of facts to which Pannone plead. That statement provides details of payments {NAME REDACTED} and Glancy; that Pannone and {NAME REDACTED} arranged for a $10,000 bribe to 'another unidentified' city official in exchange for waiving $450,000 in back taxes; and that another unidentified property owner— "an early bird taxpayer"—bribed Pannone and {NAME REDACTED} for a tax break that was granted 15 minutes before the tax board officially met on [DATE REDACTED] therefore avoiding any public opposition."

Source: FBI File FOIA request on Cianci.

In June 2000, Frank Corrente was indicted on charges of arranging bribes for city leases and contracts. The charges stemmed from allegations of fixed bids for properties leased for the school department. These led Freitas to work with the FBI.

But the biggest shock came in April 2001 with the unveiling of a sealed indictment against seven individuals.

- Vincent Cianci, Jr., Providence Mayor

- Frank Corrente, former chief of administration

- Artin H. Coloian, Cianci's Chief of Staff

- Joseph A. Pannone, ex-chairperson of the Board of Tax Assessment Review

- Richard E. Autiello, of Providence

- Edward E. Voccola, of Cranston

The ninety-seven-page, thirty-count indictment charged the defendants with racketeering, conspiracy, extortion, mail fraud, and witness tampering.

While any indictments of government political operatives draw interest, the Cianci indictment was titanic, rippling through the city and state.

The indictment alleged Cianci and his co-defendants took in more than $1.5 million during the 1990s- extorting cash and campaign contributions for leases, contracts, jobs, promotions, and other benefits.

Most of that money involved an allegedly crooked deal in which the impoverished school department paid $1.3 million (an inflated rate) to rent space in a former auto body shop owned by Edward Voccola.

Another $250,000 in campaign contributions was allegedly extorted from tow-truck operators to keep their place on the Police Department's lucrative tow list

Cianci was also charged with attempting to extort a $10,000 bribe in a city real estate deal, extorting a $10,000 bribe for a property-tax reduction, extorting a $5,000 bribe for a city job, and extorting a free lifetime membership in the exclusive University Club.

The mayor was also charged with witness tampering for allegedly trying to influence the grand jury testimony of a city official in the summer of 1999 about the University Club.

While all this was playing out in the public eye, Pat Cortellessa—and many others who'd faced the vindictiveness of the Cianci political machine—were not the least bit surprised.

For Pat, Tony Freitas, and others who'd been victimized by the rampant corruption, the looming trial would be a vindication of their efforts to reveal the true workings of Cianci.

But no one was counting Buddy out yet. If the man was anything, he was resilient and often seemed impervious to outside challenges.

Like the once reputed Teflon Don, John Gotti, Cianci had weathered many previous threats to his political survival, and many, if not most, thought he'd prevail once again.

A Long and Winding Road

The years preceding the Plunder Dome indictment saw dramatic changes in the city. The economy thrived; the business environment improved.

How much of it was attributable to Buddy Cianci is debatable. Still, there was a definite change in the city, at least downtown.

In 1982, during Cianci's first term as mayor, he had a hand in preserving the Providence Performing Arts Center, turning it into a world-class venue.

In 1994, Waterfire opened to international acclaim. The performance location was made available as part of the Providence River relocation project, reopening the long-covered rivers.

In 1999, just before the Plunder Dome matter became public, the Providence Place Mall opened.

Cianci claimed almost exclusive credit for the projects, but the truth was more complex. Some of the success was fortuitous timing, and most of it was due to the efforts of many other people.

But in keeping with the Cianci game plan, the truth didn't matter if the mayor got credit for something.

The distribution of success—and the accompanying financial benefit—wasn't equally shared throughout the city. While many changes came to the downtown area and the east side prospered, the south and west sides were ignored.

It all came down to votes and fundraising opportunities. As long as the mayor was credited with whatever development or civic improvement took place, the truth behind who was responsible didn't matter

Trial

"The greatest minds are capable of the greatest vices as well as of the greatest virtues." ~ Rene Descartes

On April 23, 2002, the trial of Vincent A. "Buddy" Cianci began in the United States District Court for the State of Rhode Island.

Presiding over the trial was Judge Ernest Torres, a Regan appointee, who assumed the bench in 1987, replacing Judge Bruce Selya, who had been nominated for the First Circuit Court of Appeals.

Torres had a reputation as a no-nonsense fair judge. However, in Cianci's book, he portrays the judge as having some animosity toward him because of a decades-long feud between Cianci and the late Senator John Chaffee, who had twice nominated Torres for the bench.

Assistant United States Attorney (AUSA) Richard Rose, representing the government, with a reputation as a tenacious prosecutor who would present a masterful case.

Cianci was represented by Richard Egbert, one of the most effective and practiced defense lawyers. Egbert had a fearless reputation and was never one to shy from challenging the government.

During almost every day of the trial, Pat Cortellessa sat in the courtroom and finally got to hear corroboration about everything he and others experienced under the Cianci administration.

There were several evidentiary matters for the judge to decide, some of which went against the mayor.

One was clearly devastating to the Cianci defense. The judge ruled against allowing the defense to play an audiotape of Cianci telling an undercover agent working for the FBI that he (Cianci) would "cut off the cojones of anyone who solicited a bribe." (Fisher, 2011)

The judge ruled it was irrelevant heresy and that the conversation "does not relate to any predicate act or to any specific matter with respect to which the government has presented evidence."

The judge concluded it was a self-serving attempt by Cianci to cover his tracks from previous acts.

Cianci, in his book *Politics and Pasta: How I Prosecuted Mobsters, Rebuilt a Dying City, Dined with Sinatra, Spent Five Years in a Federally Funded Gated Community, and Lived to Tell the Tale,* made much of what he saw as unfair treatment by the judge toward the defense.

About the judge ruling against allowing the defense playing the recording, Cianci wrote, "My attorney, Richard Egbert, one of the best defense lawyers in America, was dumbfounded by the decision." (Fisher, 2011)

Among the many witnesses testifying at the trial, one was particularly troubling. However, most of the public took little notice once the testimony was over.

Former Police Chief the late Urbano "Barney" Prignano, who'd left the department under a cloud of controversy, was a witness for the prosecution.

Up until he departed from office and his appearance at trial, Barney Prignano had an admirable, if colorful, career with the department.

He'd made some significant cases, arrested some serious bad guys, and worked in the dangerous areas of narcotics and organized crime.

He could be ascorbic at moments. But, as detailed in several publications, including Mike Stanton's book, *The Prince of Providence,* one such incident stands out.

At a pre-trial appearance at the courthouse, where he would be immunized from prosecution in exchange for his testimony, Prignano had a heated discussion with a Providence Journal reporter.

> *"Prignano accused Journal reporter Bill Malinowski of writing negative things about him because "You don't write the truth about me because my last name ends in a vowel." Malinowski pointed out that his name also ended with a vowel. Prignano said it didn't. So Malinowski spelled it for him.*

"Barney said, 'That's the wrong vowel,' Stanton recalled." (Stanton, 2003)

That such an officer, rising meteorically through the ranks, could be corrupted by Cianci says much about the tenor of the Cianci administration.

The fallout from those who benefited from the corrupted promotional process would last for years.

In May 2002, Prignano testified under immunity that as chief, he'd helped officers cheat on their promotion exams.

He also testified about the influence of City Hall on the Police Department and how Cianci and administration director Frank Corrente decided on promotions.

While the evidence of widespread corruption permeating city hall was troubling, there is none more so than casting a taint over the highly respected Providence Police Department and most of the officers who served with honor and distinction.

Often these elements of the trial are lost in the shadow of Buddy's cult of personality and the more salacious incidents of corruption.

In 2004, a report found that promotional procedures in the department "were corrupted by cheating, collusion, and political influence."

The troubling report led to significant changes within the promotion system and the retirement of some officers tainted by the corrupt practice. Moreover, it offered hope for change to the overwhelmingly honest members of the Providence Police Department.

But all of that was in the future; the trial still loomed big in the day's news, captivating the city, state, and even national media.

Even Imus reached out to Cianci during the trial. Cianci proclaimed his innocence.

Imus, never at a loss for a quick comeback, said, "You can say you're not guilty, but they can still have something on you. You would know."

Imus said he hoped the mayor would "get off." To which Buddy replied, "found not guilty." (Imus, n.d.)

The trial had moments of drama, moments of levity, and moments of stark realization that the once "anti-corruption" candidate was anything but.

Under the defense theory of the case, Cianci was as much a victim as the people of Providence.

He was duped by underlings and used as bait to solicit bribes in exchange for favorable treatment from the city.

Under the prosecution's theory, Cianci ran a fiefdom in much the same way as Raymond L. S. Patriarca. Using a wink and a nod to convey what he wanted—money—and how he wanted to be insulated from the process, thus the "self-serving" recording of him threatening to remove the "cojones" from anyone who offered him a bribe (at least directly), Cianci ran a sophisticated, organized, and politically dominant corrupt organization which controlled the city, the police department, and the day-to-day operation of city government.

The jury would face a choice between an evil genius and a duped fool. It would take seven weeks of testimony, hundreds of hours of video, myriad witnesses, and tedious recitations of financial records.

All of which painted a picture of a dangerously corrupt city administration.

None of this was news to Pat Cortellessa. The revelations weren't so much startling as they were affirmations of the things Cortellessa and others had been fighting against for years.

Having seen first-hand the machinations of Corrente and others, now confirmed by the damning recordings made of Corrente and others directly soliciting bribes using the mayor's name, was exhilarating.

There was never any doubt in Pat Cortellessa's mind that the jury *should* convict Cianci.

However, he doubted whether they *would* convict him.

Pat decided to take a playbook out of the John Gotti trial in New York. Supporters of Gotti plastered the surrounding streets and area of the courthouse with placards and signs attesting to Gotti's good character and upstanding nature, hoping to sway the jury.

Pat took a similar approach to counteract the vocal and noisy Cianci supporters around the courthouse.

He posted signs, published ads in the Providence Journal, and spoke to any of the many media outlets who would put him on.

He also tried to be at the trial whenever possible, positioning himself to make sure Cianci saw him.

Pat's incessant in-your-face aggravation of Cianci started long before the trial itself. At Cianci's initial arraignment, to counteract the crowd of loyal Cianci supporters, Pat arranged for a dozen guys to be outside the courtroom chanting, "Cianci, step down! Cianci, step down!"

The chanting chorus—enticed from Traveler's Aid for $20 and a sandwich at Mark's Deli—followed Cianci and his attorney, Richard Egbert, all the way to the mayor's limousine.

Some might think it petty, but after enduring years of political interference into his business matters and suspecting others faced the same issues, the trial offered not a sense of satisfaction at seeing the mayor on trial, but confirmation the system works and corruption will be rooted out.

Pat wasn't the only one with an in-your-face presence during Cianci's trial. John DePetro, the acerbic, witty, and often insightful radio talk show host and consistent Cianci critic, set up a broadcast trailer outside the courthouse and did a virtual play-by-play of the trial's progress.

Pat was a frequent guest on the John DePetro show, and the talk show host offered the public a constant flood of trial updates and news tidbits.

While Cianci lived for the spotlight, this was the kind of illumination on the mayor he would prefer to avoid. DePetro was relentless in pursuing the mayor and had been for most of Cianci's time in office.

DePetro was a constant critic of the many controversies swirling around the mayor, and covering the trial offered a crowning achievement for the show.

Pat's frequent attendance at the trial provided DePetro with plenty of fodder for discussion. As the trial drew to its conclusion and the anticipation of a verdict drew closer, the media storm grew to a crescendo.

The mayor supporters and critics were equally vociferous in their perspectives on the mayor's chances before the jury.

With the testimony at an end, and the Judge preparing his remarks before charging the jury, the atmosphere around the courthouse was electric.

All that remained was for the twelve members of the jury of his peers to deliberate the mayor's fate.

Verdict

On June 24, 2002, the jury in the matter of the United States of America v. Vincent A. Cianci, Jr. filed into the courtroom.

The jury's forewoman handed the verdict sheet to the court clerk, who took his position at the lectern.

Pat Cortellessa and Tony Freitas sat in the front row, occasionally catching Cianci's eye. Pat couldn't suppress a smile; no matter what happened in the next few moments, he felt they made their point. No one was above the law.

From his vantage point, Pat could see Cianci's hands trembling. On the defense table in front of Cianci rested the verdict sheet. Cianci grabbed a pen and focused on the paper, never raising his eyes toward the clerk.

"Count One, racketeering conspiracy, as to Vincent A. Cianci, Jr, — GUILTY."

Buddy never raised his head, following along as the clerk read off the other charges against the mayor, all NOT GUILTY, except for one deadlocked verdict on the extortion charge over the University Club membership.

The judge sent the jury back to continue deliberations on the deadlocked verdict. For several hours, the jurors who had voted to acquit Cianci on the extortion charge worked to change the vote of the three holdouts.

Eventually, by convincing the three they had convicted Cianci of the most serious charge—the RICO Conspiracy count—the jurors returned with a verdict of not guilty.

Of the twenty-six charges against Cianci, he was acquitted of twenty-five and convicted on one. That one count, an affirmation of all the allegations of corruption within the Cianci administration, would be enough to end the mayor's political career.

In the end, the jury believed the Government. The evidence showed Cianci was intelligent, cautious, and adept at avoiding direct involvement. The evidence showing he knew what was going on was indisputable.

From the jury's verdict on the one count of RICO Conspiracy, one can draw a reasonable inference. The jurors recognized Cianci for what he was, a brilliant but flawed individual caught up in the seductive power of politics and the driving need for money.

Through AUSA Richard Rose, the government had proven beyond a reasonable doubt the Vincent A. "Buddy" Cianci was guilty of controlling a Racketeer Influenced and Corrupt Organization using the power of city government as his platform.

The judge set a sentencing date for September.

Passing Sentence

On September 6, 2002, former Mayor Vincent A. "Buddy" Cianci stood before Judge Torres. The reality of his conviction could longer be shielded by Cianci's affable sense of humor and quick wit.

He was just another convicted felon and corrupt politician in what is sadly a long line of such individuals in Rhode Island history.

The Judge did not mince his words, but he did characterize the man before him as an enigma.

> *"I'm struck between the parallels between this case and the classic story of Dr. Jekyll and Mr. Hyde.*
>
> *"There appear to be two very different Buddy Ciancis that came across. The first is a skilled and charismatic political figure, probably one of the most talented politicians Rhode Island has ever seen, someone with wit, who thinks quickly on his feet and can enthrall an audience.*

"The second Buddy Cianci presided over an administration that is rife with corruption at all levels and engaged in an egregious breach of public trust by engaging to operate the city that Buddy Cianci was supposed to serve as a criminal enterprise to line his own pockets."

Pausing for a moment to look directly at Cianci, Judge Torres continued.

"My job is to sentence the second Buddy Cianci because the first Buddy Cianci wouldn't be here."

On the charge of Racketeering Conspiracy, Judge Torres sentenced Cianci to fifty-four months in federal prison.

But like many years of Buddy's reign in Providence, there was a bit of a surprise.

In Mike Stanton's book, *The Prince of Providence,* he describes the unexpected twist.

"But Cianci did not go gently. The judge had one final surprise. He gave Cianci a ninety-day stay of execution, allowing

him to ask the First Circuit Court of Appeals to permit him to remain free during his appeal. As Cianci left the courthouse, legal minds raced to digest the consequences of the stay of execution. The city charter called for Cianci to lose office upon sentencing. But if the judge delayed execution of the sentence, did that mean Cianci was legally out of office? (Stanton, 2003)

The judge's stay set the city into a tizzy. Cianci, walking out of the courthouse, said he was still mayor. The city's legal counsel entered into tense, often angry, negotiations with John Lombardi, the President of the City Council who would assume the title of mayor on Cianci's removal from office.

Uncertainty roiled the city. Cianci, never known for fearing a fight, argued he should retain the office. However, Lombardi and his allies wanted this finished, and Cianci gone.

But by the afternoon, with the police honor guard ready to accompany Lombardi into the swearing-in ceremony, Cianci surrendered to the inevitable and accepted his fate.

In Stanton's book, he relates an aside after the mayor became just another citizen. The Tuesday following his exit from office, the former mayor was having his hair done.

> *"Michael Corrente, who knew the (salon) owner, called to chat. Corrente, who was planning on making a movie about Cianci's life, soon found himself on the phone with the ex-mayor.*
>
> *'The judge cut me some slack,' Cianci said.*
>
> *'I heard,' replied Corrente.*
>
> *The mayor chuckled. 'Dr. Jekyll and Mr. Hyde. Dr. Jekyll and Mr. Hyde. The cocksucker. He didn't give me two fucking paychecks, though."* (Stanton, 2003)

Buddy remained Buddy despite it all.

Whether such a stay would be granted to the "ordinary" defendant before the court is debatable, but Cianci was hardly an "ordinary" defendant.

In the end, it didn't matter. The appeal to the First Circuit was denied, and Cianci now faced the uncertainty and reality of a federal prison.

Aftermath

Once the dust settled and the now-former mayor was off to prison, more startling information bubbled into the public eye.

Troubling information came out of the FBI on other issues discovered during the investigation.

> *During the course of the investigation it was determined that the Providence Police Department had been rigging the promotional process for the rank of captain and above with the purpose of rewarding significant fundraisers for and contributed to Mayor Cianci.*
>
> *Special agents conducted a complicated detailed analysis of all the promotional records of the Providence Police Department and we're able to determine that every promotional process for the rank of Sergeant and above had been rigged for the past seven years.*

As a result of the investigation, the Providence police union has taken steps to correct the deficiencies in the promotional system. The facts of that investigation have been forwarded to the Rhode Island attorney general for prosecution.

The full extent and reach of corruption will probably never be known. Forever silenced by the death of Buddy Cianci shortly after his third attempt—and only failure—to reclaim the mayor's office.

During this last run, Buddy made what many would see as an attempt at a mea culpa to correct past errors. While he never acknowledged his guilt in the matter—claiming that he was convicted for being in charge"—he recognized the need to present a changed Buddy to the world.

He enlisted the help of several influential individuals in trying to recruit honest and credible individuals into any new Cianci administration.

In the book, *It's Just the Way It Was: Inside the War on the New England Mob and other stories* by Joe

Broadmeadow and Brendan Doherty, former superintendent of the Rhode Island State Police, *Doherty* details the extent Cianci went to convince him to accept a position as Director of Administration.

> *In August of that year, I got a cold call from him. He told me he was up in the polls and could win the election, but the media kept attacking him on his past indiscretions. They harped on the fact this would just be another corrupt political administration. He tried to convince me his past "shenanigans" were just that, in the past. He wanted me to know that. There was a slight desperation to his tone.*

> *By this point, I had retired from the State Police and run unsuccessfully for U.S. Congress. But I think, when all was said and done, my reputation remained intact. I fared well in a poll for governor, which I did not pursue. I*

had political options but pursued other interests.

First, Buddy told me how well he was doing. Then he said his advisory committee believed the campaign needed a game-changer. They agreed one guy fit the bill. I asked why he was explaining this to me, searching for a way out of the inevitable. I tried to beat him to the punch. I wished him well but said I couldn't get involved in his campaign.

I was trying to deflect, pivot, and maneuver my way out of what I knew was coming next, but Buddy would not be derailed.

"You're the game-changer," he said. "You're the guy people trust. They know you wouldn't allow any wheeling and dealing."

I'll never forget that call because it was sad.

"Colonel," he continued, "I need to be able to report that you will be the Director of Administration."

Frankly, I would have loved to run the city, but I'm not naive. I know what would happen if I agreed. The first time I told him I would handle all finances in the city, contracts, or other matters involving money, I'd force him to fire me.

I'll admit, I gave it some thought. I knew I could run the city ethically, but I also knew from my familiarity with Buddy's history that when there were contracts to award, he'd try to interfere.

Even if it were legitimate, the appearance of impropriety would be too disturbing for me. The optics of working for Buddy would disappoint many people. I needed to maintain my reputation for the troopers who used to work for me, the organization, and the people throughout the state who believed in me. I knew I could have helped him, and probably kept him straight, but it was a matter of appearances.

Perception is reality.

I politely told him no, but he wouldn't accept it. No is not a word Buddy understood when it applied to something he wanted.

He had friends call me. He even got to my brother Chris. Chris knew Buddy through their mutual friendship with former Boston Mayor Raymond Flynn. Ray was the former Ambassador to the Vatican and a family friend. Buddy put Joe Paolino on the mission. Joe was the former Mayor of Providence and another pal of Ray Flynn's. Joe was also the Ambassador to Malta and a successful businessman in Providence.

169

Buddy was relentless.

(Excerpt from Its Just the Way It Was: Inside the War on the New England Mob by Joe Broadmeadow and Brendan Doherty.) (Broadmeadow, It's Just the Way It Was: Inside the War on the New England Mob and other stories, 2019)

Cortellessa and others were not content to let the past stay in the past. On the contrary, they made it very clear their mission was to remind the voters of the real Buddy Cianci and how a return to the "good ole' days" was a recipe for disaster.

Pat contacted his old friend, Tony Freitas, and strategized to derail Cianci's 2014 re-election campaign.

Cortellessa and Freitas went to every mayoral debate, went on TV and radio, and did everything they could to work against Buddy's return to the office of mayor.

Cortellessa and Freitas would position themselves at the debates so Cianci would see them as he responded to questions.

During one debate, things took a turn for the bizarre.

During one debate, Cianci supporters openly jostled with Cortellessa and others. One woman approached Pat and grabbed at the signs about Cianci's corruption.

Pat walked away, but it was hardly the end of the incident.

The woman filed a complaint for assault with the police department, and Cortellessa was charged. However, there were many witnesses to the incident who contradicted the woman's claim.

Cianci, alleging Cortellessa was a paid member of then-candidate Elorza's campaign, held a press conference saying the Elorza campaign should fire Cortellessa.

Elorza denied Cortellessa was part of the campaign but merely a supporter. The campaign took a turn for the ugly.

Pat refused to accept any plea agreement and went to trial over the assault. However, after hearing many witnesses testify that the woman was the instigator and that Pat never assaulted her, the case was dismissed.

Judge Capraro made a point of chastising the city for even bring the case to court. He called the case "Providence Politics at its best."

In the end, Cianci lost the election by seven points, and Elorza became mayor.

With the loss in 2014, Buddy's political career and influence for better or worse in the city were over. But, unfortunately, the damage he'd done to people like Pat Cortellessa and others would not soon be forgotten, and the many good things would fade away.

At one of his last appearances, Buddy remained as he always was for the controversial unveiling of his official mayoral portrait.

Despite everything that had happened- removed from office twice, five years in federal prison, an unfamiliar loss in running for mayor—Cianci maintained his sense of humor.

As his portrait was unveiled, he quipped, "It's not the first time I've been framed."

The City of Providence under Cianci, and to some extent even in his absence from the mayor's office, was much like Jekyll and Hyde, as the judge once asserted after Cianci's conviction.

There was the downtown revitalization for which Buddy claimed exclusive credit, and there was the reality that the city was in deep financial trouble. Moreover, pension benefits, agreed to by Cianci in exchange for the expected political support, threatened the very viability of the city.

Corrupt practices cost precious tax dollars, all to the detriment of city residents and taxpayers. The school department wasted precious money lining the pockets of a few well-connected individuals as the education of its youth deteriorated.

The taint of cronyism poisoned the reputations of the many good men and women of the police department who knew well that some were gaining underserved promotions for which they were unqualified.

The reality is that the cult of personality of Buddy Cianci could no longer hide the decaying infrastructure of the city, the efforts of its many dedicated employees who refused to play politics, and the inevitable demise of the once invincible mayor.

Mr. Hyde surfaced from the dark shadows and forever obliterated Dr. Jekyll.

Pat Cortellessa had been a witness to it all. From the affable Buddy glad-handing the young club owner and encouraging him to open more businesses—while keeping the contributions to the Cianci campaign flowing—to the vindictive and vicious Buddy intolerant of any challengers.

Pat's past experiences navigating his way among the sharks and wiseguys prepared him well for his later confrontations with Cianci.

He'd learned to walk the fine line of business reality in a city that essentially had two governments, one elected and one equally powerful with no legitimacy.

Each suffered from a lack of scruples.

He survived to see the day when justice prevailed. Some might see Buddy as a victim of an overzealous FBI intent on his downfall. They will claim Buddy saved Providence.

But Pat Cortellessa knows better. He knows honest people are the foundation of government and need protection from those who would subvert the system for their own purposes.

While Buddy did many good things for the city, motive matters. There was always some residual benefit to the mayor, no matter how insignificant, that, over time, corroded the system from within.

The stories revealed in this book tell a different tale than the one many people want to accept. But the reality is it is all true.

It played out in the clubs and bars in the city.

It played out in land and licensing deals.

It played out in $1000 per ticket fundraisers.

And finally, it played out in the Plunder Dome trial for all to see.

Buddy may have made light that he was convicted for "being in charge," but that is what he was elected to do. And if those around him corrupted the system, he bears the burden of his failure to stop it.

Pat Cortellessa, and others, paid a high price for opposing and exposing corruption. The City of Providence and the State of Rhode Island are better off because some took such a stance

The Image of Politics

Pat and Governor DiPrete at the opening of Cafe Plaza

Buddy victory party 1990

Buddy presenting an award to Pat for Café Providence

Pat and Kristen Cortellessa, and Buddy at Nobody Café building 1992e

Providence Journal story on campaign signatures

Providence Journal Story on Signature Challenges

Joe Broadmeadow and Pat Cortellessa

EDITION

Supreme Court justice blocks eviction of Cafe Plaza operator

■ The ruling allows Pat Cortellessa to pursue an appeal in his legal battle with the city.

By GREGORY SMITH
Journal-Bulletin Staff Writer

PROVIDENCE — The "open" flag continues to fly above Cafe Plaza, which has won another stay of execution.

Supreme Court Justice Robert G. Flanders has blocked for the time being any attempt by the city to evict the operator of Cafe Plaza, Pat Cortellessa. Cortellessa has been skirmishing with the city for more than a year over his right to stay in the comfort station-turned-restaurant and bar in Kennedy Plaza. The city owns the cafe building and Cortellessa's company leases it.

Cortellessa thus wins an opportunity to press a potentially time-consuming appeal in Supreme Court. He is trying to persuade the court to issue a writ of certiorari — a ruling that it will consider the merits of his case.

The flamboyant Cortellessa, meanwhile, has hung a sign in a storefront that he owns on Washington Street, a half-block away from City Hall, announcing that it is "Cortellessa for Mayor of Providence Headquarters." The next mayoral election is not scheduled until 1998.

Asked if he is trying to tweak Mayor Vincent A. Cianci Jr., Cortellessa yesterday replied, "It's very possible that the 'tweaking' will (evolve into) a top-notch, high-intensity campaign for mayor of Providence. It's not a stunt. It's something I believe in."

Cianci is chairman of the Board of Park Commissioners, which controls has the cafe building.

Starting a campaign six months before an election won't suffice if he intends to win, Cortellessa said. He

needs at least two years or 20 months to introduce himself to voters and influential individuals and to take soundings of his potential political support, he said.

Cortellessa, who said he would seek election as an independent if he runs, said he sat in on Monday's City Council meeting to begin the process of familiarization.

Regarding the lease dispute, the city last spring won a judgment against Cortellessa in District Court, in which the court said he could be evicted because his lease had expired. The court ordered him to pay $23,000 in disputed rent and interest.

When Cortellessa appealed to Superior Court, Judge Thomas H. Needham dismissed the appeal. The judge concluded that Cortellessa failed to pay his monthly rent on time during the appeal period, which is grounds for immediate dismissal of an eviction appeal. It is that dismissal that Cortellessa wants the Supreme Court to overturn.

If Flanders had not issued a stay, the city could have had Cortellessa evicted and the attempted appeal to Supreme Court might have been moot.

Lauren E. Jones, lawyer for Cafe Plaza, said the justice granted his request for a stay "because denying a stay would alter the status quo" and Cortellessa would "literally be out on the street" without having his plea heard.

City Solicitor Charles R. Mansolillo said the stay was granted only because the full high court is unlikely to consider the writ of certiorari "possibly as early as this week. It isn't something that sets us (city) back a good deal," the solicitor commented.

The issue that the Supreme Court is being asked to consider centers on the deadline for cafe rent payments. City lawyers say the rent

was due on the first business day of every month and that Cortellessa made late payments while his Superior Court appeal was pending. Jones contends that Cortellessa had a 15-day grace period and that he paid within that period.

Cortellessa has taken his fight to the court of public opinion, as well. He led a rally and a petition drive that garnered 1,632 signatures in support of his request for a public hearing of the dispute by the Board of Park Commissioners. Officials rejected the petition and refused to call a hearing.

Cortellessa has continued to pay rent and operate the cafe, although his lease expired in 1995; he disputes the expiration. City officials recently have allowed him to stay in order to keep the building occupied until they found a new operator. Cortellessa, meanwhile, moved his fight to Supreme Court.

But the city apparently has been preparing to evict Cortellessa because it began advertising for a new restaurant operator and it refused his rent payment for October. Under the Supreme Court stay, Cortellessa yesterday paid his $3,000 rent for October to the city Law Department.

Nancy L. Derrig, city parks superintendent, said last month that the city wants the location to be a "nice restaurant." As a Cortellessa enterprise, "It's much more of a music place — a bar," she said. It "caters to a young crowd, a drinking crowd." Derrig said the city also objects to Cortellessa's use of the rear portion of his building as a coffee takeout counter, because the lease does not provide for that and the city wants to discourage takeouts.

The city, however, also will consider proposals from bidders for a use other than a restaurant, she said.

181

Buddy telling Pat to run as a Republican

Image 1Cafe Plaza where the conversation took place

Buddy's photo, which hung in every office in City Hall

FD-302 (Rev. 10-6-95)

- 1 -

FEDERAL BUREAU OF INVESTIGATION

Date of transcription   09/30/1999

PASQUALE VINCENT CORTELLESSA, White/Male, Date of Birth: July 29, 1956, was contacted and advised of the official identity of the interviewing Agents. CORTELLESSA had previously been interviewed relative to the CAFE PLAZA on April 9, 1996. CORTELLESSA thereafter provided the following information:

In or around 1991, CORTELLESSA wanted to put a DUNKIN DONUT franchise in the CAFE PLAZA building at KENNEDY PLAZA. CORTELLESSA ran the idea past MAYOR VINCENT CIANCI who gave CORTELLESSA a verbal "okay" to pursue the DUNKIN DONUT franchise.

CORTELLESSA was subsequently contacted by Providence businessman [   ] who told CORTELLESSA that he was interested in buying the CAFE PLAZA and putting in a [   ] franchise at that location. CORTELLESSA subsequently met with [   ] Telephone [   ] was the individual who was going to put the franchise in the CAFE PLAZA if [   ] purchased the business from CORTELLESSA.   b6 b7c

In a meeting that occurred between CORTELLESSA and [   ] [   ] told CORTELLESSA did not like putting money in paper bags. [   ] stated that [   ] would handle that end. CORTELLESSA understood this to mean that cash payoffs would have to be made to public officials in order to facilitate the [   ] franchise being allowed at KENNEDY PLAZA.   b6 b7c

[   ] subsequently offered CORTELLESSA approximately $125,000.00 for the CAFE PLAZA business and CORTELLESSA turned him down.   NMU

No DUNKIN DONUTS [   ] franchise was ever put in the CAFE PLAZA building.

CORTELLESSA has heard several bits of information on the street relative to former CIANCI aide [   ] was building a house in [   ] CORTELLESSA has heard that workers from the [   ] CONSTRUCTION COMPANY worked on [   ] home while they were   b6 b7c

Investigation on   9/28/99   at   Providence, Rhode Island

File # 194B-BS-81295   Date dictated   9/29/99

by

This document contains neither recommendations nor conclusions of the FBI. It is the property of the FBI and is loaned to your agency; it and its contents are not to be distributed outside your agency.

Image from FBI File of Interview with Pat Cortellessa

184

FD-302a (Rev. 10-6-95)

194B-BS-81295

Continuation of FD-302 of ___PASQUALE VINCENT CORTELLESSA___ , On _9/28/99_ , Page __2__

supposed to be doing work on the construction of the FLEET SKATING
CENTER.

In addition, CORTELLESSA has heard several rumors
relative to an illegal or questionable sewer hookup at [   ]   b6
new residence. While at [   ] construction site, CORTELLESSA   b7c
saw a dumpster which he believed to be owned by a City vendor.

CORTELLESSA supplied photocopies of documents relative to
the DUNKIN DONUTS CAFE PLAZA issue as well as the failure of the
city to renew his lease at the CAFE PLAZA in 1995. The details of
that were previously furnished by CORTELLESSA in his April 1996
interview contained in 194C-BS-71217 Serial 197.

These photocopies are attached and incorporated herein.

Image from FBI Files

185

Tony Freitas, whose work with the FBI took down Cianci

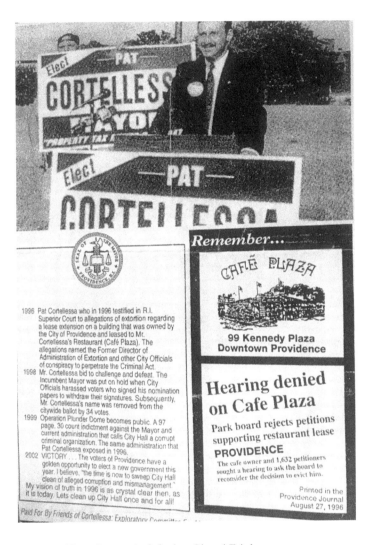

Flyer Pat posted during Cianci Trial

Front Page of the list of charges in the Plunder Dome trial

7-21-98 I had a phone call from
dein cated asking me If I sign pat Cortellessia
paper I said yes. They ask me if I was forced
to sign. I said no. They said that they were
coming by to see me to sign a paper saying
that I am free of the whole thing. they
call me from a cellar phone to say that
they were down stairs on my porch.
I went down stairs and ask them If I sign
that paper I wouldn't have anything to do
with the poll. They said yes. So I sign 7-22-98
I got another phone asking me If I sign
papers from pat I said yes. about hour later
channel 10 came by asking me question about what
went on about 7-21-98 I told them want they and
also mine voting right was volilated by false hood
By Dottie Colon and I want to revoke my
Affidavit I signed on 7-22-98

State of Rhode Island and ...
My Commission Expires December 4, 2001

Letter refuting the claim of signature fraud (Identifying information redacted)

189

UNITED STATES DISTRICT COURT
FOR THE DISTRICT OF RHODE ISLAND

UNITED STATES OF AMERICA

v.   CR. No. 00-083-T

VINCENT A. CIANCI, JR. a/k/a
"BUDDY;" FRANK E. CORRENTE; and
RICHARD E. AUTIELLO

VERDICT FORM

WE, THE JURY, find as follows:

COUNT I - RICO CONSPIRACY
18 U.S.C. § 1962(d)

VINCENT A. CIANCI, JR.

GUILTY _____   NOT GUILTY _____

FRANK E. CORRENTE

GUILTY _____   NOT GUILTY _____

RICHARD E. AUTIELLO

GUILTY _____   NOT GUILTY _____

COUNT II - RICO
18 U.S.C. § 1962(c)

VINCENT A. CIANCI, JR.

GUILTY _____   NOT GUILTY _____

If you find defendant CIANCI guilty as to Count Two,
please indicate which two or more of the following
Racketeering Acts have been proven:

Racketeering Act 5   YES ___   NO ___

If you find that Racketeering Act 5 has been

Pat Presenting his case at Secretary of State Debate

Pat and his wife Kristin at a debate

Billboard for Senate District 27 Campaign 2020

Secretary of State Campaign Team 2018

Pat at campaign event 2018 Secretary of State

e

About the Authors: Pat Cortellessa

After working to defeat Buddy Cianci in the 2014 mayoral election, Pat set his sights on other political offices.

In 2018, he ran as the endorsed Republican candidate for Secretary of State against Democrat Nellie Gorbea.

In 2020, he ran as the endorsed Republican candidate for Senate District 27 against Democrat Hanna Gallo.

Never taking his eyes off politics, he is still active. Pat is the head of security for TPG Hotel Group Headquarters in Cranston, R.I.

He lives in Cranston with his wife, Kristin. He has three children, Vincent, Alex, and Joelle, and a grandson, Anthony.

His passion for the political arena and challenging those who use the system for their own benefit has never wavered.

About the Authors: Joe Broadmeadow

Joe Broadmeadow retired with the rank of Captain from the East Providence, Rhode Island Police Department after twenty years. He served in the various divisions within the department, including Commander of Investigative Services. He also worked in the Organized Crime Drug Enforcement Task Force (OCDETF) and on special assignment to the FBI Drug Task Force.

***Divine Providence: The Mayor, The Mob, and The Man in the Middle* is the fourth non-fiction book by Joe Broadmeadow.**

It's Just the Way It Was: Inside the War on the New England Mob and other stories, UnMade: Honor Loyalty Redemption (written with Bobby Walason) and ***Choices: You Make 'em You Own 'em,*** *(The Jerry Tillinghast Story),* Joe's first three non-fiction works, were Number 1 New Releases on Amazon.

And there are more intriguing projects on the way.

Joe is the author of several novels. **Silenced Justice** and **Collision Course,** featuring East Providence Police Detective Lieutenant Josh Williams, and **A Change of Hate**, a spin-off of the Josh Williams series, featuring Defense Attorney Harrison 'Hawk' Bennett.

The books continue to garner rave reviews and are available on Amazon, Barnes & Noble, and bookstores everywhere.

When Joe is not writing, he is hiking or fishing (and thinking about writing). Joe completed a 2,185-mile thru-hike of the Appalachian Trail in September 2014. After completing the trail, Joe published a short story, **Spirit of the Trail**, available on Amazon.

He lives in Rhode Island with his wife, Susan, just a short distance from their daughter, Kelsey, her husband, Chuck, and the amazingly intriguing grandson, Levi David. And, of course, Seamus, who does not realize he is a dog.

Thanks for reading! Please take a moment to review the book; it is most appreciated.

https://www.amazon.com/Joe-Broadmeadow/e/B00OWPE9GU

Contact the author:
joe.broadmeadow@jebwizardpublishing.com

Website: www.jebwizardpublishing.com

Twitter: @JBroadmeadow

Author Blog: www.joebroadmeadowblog.com

Works Cited

Broadmeadow, J. (2019). *It's Just the Way It Was: Inside the War on the New England Mob and other stories.* Providence: JEBWizard Publishing.

Broadmeadow, J. (2021). *Legendary Speaking.* Providence: JEBWizard Publishing.

Fisher, V. A. (2011). *Politics and Pasta: How I Prosecuted Mobsters, Rebuilt a Dying City, Dined with Sinatra, Spent Five Years in a Federally Funded Gated Community, and Lived to Tell the Tale.* Providence: Thomas Dunne Books.

Haupt, K. D. (1982). *Lost in the Iron Triangle:Public Policymaking in Rhode Island (Open Master's Theses Paper 512.* Retrieved from University of Rhode Island: https://digitalcommons.uri.edu/theses/512

Imus, D. (n.d.). *Crimetown (Season 1)*. Retrieved from Vimeo: https://vimeo.com/215247517

Mikovits, A. (n.d.). Former Chief Urbano Prignano Dies. *Providence Journal*, pp. https://www.providencejournal.com/news/20171122/former-providence-police-chief-urbano-prignano-dies.

Stanton, M. (2003). *The Prince of Providence.* New York: Random House.

WPRI 12, S. D. (2021, May 21). *WPRI.COM 12.* Retrieved from WPRI.com: https://www.wpri.com/news/local-news/providence/somebody-can-resolve-this-detectives-still-searching-for-suspects-in-1984-murder-of-providence-bar-owner/

Name Index

H

Hanrahan, Kevin · 54, 55, 56, 76

I

Imus, Don · 24, 154, 202

K

Keeler, Charles"Sonny" · 77, 80

Kent, Mike · 74, 75, 105

Kerr, Bob · 53

Kilberg, Arnold · 110

Krasnoff, Charles · 45, 46, 47

L

Lemonthe, Roland · 30

Lombardi, John · iii, 106, 165

Loqa, Ramzi · 81

M

Marfeo, Blaise · 58

Marrapese, Frank "Bobo" · 10, 12, 19, 32, 33

McCabe, Richard · 82

McElroy, Ronald · 39

McLaughlin, Patricia · 72

Mirabella, Anthony "The Moron" · 38

Mitrelis, Solon · 69

Montrond, Sonny · 79

Moran, Chris · 59, 62, 63

S

Salemme, Frank \ ·
78

Salemme, Frank Jr ·
78

Scivola, Chippy · 56

Selya, Bruce Judge ·
149

Sinatra, Frank · 2

St. Laurent, Anthony ·
105

Stanton, Mike · 152,
164

T

Thibeault, Bob · 33

Tillinghast, Jerry · 10,
14, 18, 199

Tippett, Andre · 40

Torres, Ernest Judge ·
ii, 149

V

Vickers, Jimmy · 54,
59

Vigeant, Billy "Billy V"
· 52

Viola, Frank · 80, 81,
82

Violet, Arlene
Attorney General ·
127

Voccola, Edward ·
140, 144, 145

W

Walason, Bobby · 34,
79, 199

Wilkins, Peter · 11

Winter. Howie · 83

c

CPSIA information can be obtained
at www.ICGtesting.com
Printed in the USA
BVHW051153250821
615140BV00015B/721